GPS Systems

Technology, Operation, and Applications

3rd Edition

Ben Levitan
Lawrence Harte

DiscoverNet Publishing
2474 Walnut Street, Suite 105
Cary, NC 27518 USA
Telephone: 1-301-0109
Fax: 1-919-557-2261
email: info@discovernet.com
web: www.DiscoverNet.com

DiscoverNet

Third Printing

Printed and Bound by Lightning Source, TN.

Every effort has been made to make this manual as complete and as accurate as possible. However, there may be mistakes both typographical and in content. Therefore, this text should be used only as a general guide and not as the ultimate source of information. Furthermore, this manual contains information on telecommunications accurate only up to the printing date. The purpose of this manual to educate. The authors and DiscoverNet Publishing shall have neither liability nor responsibility to any person or entity with respect to any loss or damage caused, or alleged to be caused, directly or indirectly by the information contained in this book.

International Standard Book Number: 978-193281319-7

About the Authors

Mr. Levitan is an engineer and an expert on technical standards for satellite, cellular and land mobile radio (LMR) systems including CDMA, GSM, and LTE systems. He holds 30 patents and four trade secrets in the area the wireless and GPS technologies. His expertise includes international roaming for cellular systems, wiretap standards (CALEA), local number portability, and 911 emergency standards. Mr. Levitan is an active participant for the US and international development of Cellular Telecommunications, Interstandard roaming and FCC and US government mandated features and requirements. He has represented COMSAT, Intelsat and Aeronautical Radio, Inc. in the development of satellite standards. He acts as an expert witness in patent infringement matters related to satellite, telecommunications matters. He is a frequent guest on national TV show as a telecommunications expert having appeared on all the major networks including CNN, MSNBC, NBC, ABC and HLN. Mr. Levitan can be contacted at BenLev@AOL.com. www.ThatCellPhoneGuy.com

Mr. Harte is a telecommunications expert and managing director of DiscoverNet Media. He is an inventor of 5 patents on wireless signaling and has been a voting member of the Telecommunications industry association (TIA) standards committees. Mr. Harte has worked for Ericsson/GE, Audiovox/Toshiba and Westinghouse and has been an expert consultant for Samsung, Google, Nokia, and other companies. He has developed and instructed courses for Global Knowledge, Wray Castle, and other training companies. He creates and presents the New Technology sessions at International Wireless Communication Expo (IWCE) trade show each year. As of 2016, he authored over 113 books on communication technologies on wireless, telecom, and digital media. Mr. Harte holds many degrees and certificates including an Executive MBA from Wake Forest University (1995) and a BSET from the University of the State of New York, (1990). Mr. Harte can be contacted at LHarte@LawrenceHarte.com.

Table of Contents

Preface

Location, Location, Location

"Where am I?" is probably the most frequently asked question in the human language. The real estate business lives by the motto "location, location, location". Businesses depend on the location of people and assets for revenue creation and loss prevention.

Mankind's obsession with determining location is not new. To comprehend this Quick Course, it's important to note that GPS is simply the most advanced system in the determination of location that exists today. This book will provide a thorough understanding of what the Global Positioning System (GPS) is and how it works. But more importantly, you will learn that GPS is simply a technology that enables the development of a systematic and extremely accurate determination of the position of people and assets relative to each other in a matter of milliseconds.

GPS is more than just a simple device. GPS is a tool that can be used to determine physical positions in a relative manner when used as part of an application. GPS is not useful when used by itself. The tremendous growth in the use of applications that depend on accurate knowledge of location can be largely attributed to GPS, which has all but replaced most other location technologies that have been applied.

Today's GPS devices have relatively low cost, provide high accuracy and can process position information quickly, which enhances or enables many new applications. For example, devices that provide turn-by-turn driving directions would not be possible without GPS chips that quickly determine location. Rental cars now come standard with turn-by-turn driving directions due to the speed and accuracy of GPS in the driving direction application. This application was not possible prior to the advent of GPS because a

Sexton pointed at the North Star could not efficiently provide driving direction at 60 MPH.

Devices and applications that can be "location aware" provide completely new avenues of features and services. GPS, the newest of technologies that provide location, has generated a completely new range of possibilities. GPS is not a device; it is a capability that enables applications that need location to be useful. Today, GPS chips are a crucial element when a company wishes to build a navigation device. The navigation device has existed for centuries and will continue to exist for years to come. When we speak about GPS as a system, we truly mean that determining location requires more than just a chip. As you will understand, a GPS chip is a simple receiver that receives radio signals from multiple satellites in orbit. The GPS system is dependent on the continued availability of GPS satellites to make location determination possible.

The methods used to determine one's relative position on earth are numerous, each an improvement over its predecessor. Crude maps found in caves gave way to more accurate maps as measurement sticks were devised. Those maps themselves were improved when the compass was invented. The use of the stars improved maps and navigation again, as did radar systems, aerial photography and satellite photos. Today, the best method to determine a current location is through the use of the GPS system.

GPS Executive Summary

Global Positioning Systems enable determination of a user's location on earth to an accuracy of less than a meter in a matter of milliseconds. GPS systems are realized via a network of 24 or more orbiting satellites that continuously rotate the Earth in a north to south pattern transmitting their known positions above Earth and a timestamp of their broadcast that is extremely accurate. The transmitted reports can be received by simple radio receivers which today exist as small semiconductors. There is no interaction between the device and satellites so an unlimited number of users can be served. The transmission from four satellites is necessary to determine position, which is accomplished through the use of time differential of arrival and trilateration. Time differential of arrival (TDOA) is the time difference between when a satellite sends a signal and when the signal is received by a GPS receiver. Using the received time and satellite's known location, and the known current time, a microprocessor within the GPS device can calculate its position using the simple formula of rate x time = distance. Trilateration is a form of triangulation which determines the position of a receiver by measuring its distance from three known points. The signals from three satellites are required to determine location but a forth is required to account for altitude. Trilateration is three dimensional triangulation.

By making multiple calculations using multiple satellites the accuracy of a GPS's location on Earth can be measured within a meter or less. These measurements can be calculated in milliseconds allowing a GPS device to make measurements on a continuous basis, thus allowing a user to enjoy real-time tracking of their location. With the simple formula of rate x time = distance, a GPS device can provide a user with position, velocity and direction. GPS devices translate position into longitude and latitude, a standard method of defining points on Earth, so that GPS positions can be combined with readily available maps and databases to provide turn-by-turn directions and locations of known sites such as businesses and addresses.

A Brief History of Location

From a historical standpoint, we can begin looking at navigation in 1492, because this is the period of time when man began to explore the Earth by sea and, by necessity, developed the methods and tools used for creating maps, determining location and navigating. Christopher Columbus was one of the keenest navigators of his time. His techniques were not much different than the techniques used in GPS. On September 10, 1492 Christopher Columbus was crossing the Atlantic and annotating his ship's log with its current position upon uncharted territory. He believed the Earth to be a sphere although, to this day, there are those who refute this (the Flat Earth Society www.theflatearthsociety.org). Columbus refined the techniques and tools for location determination.

The sailors in those times used two kinds of navigation methods; celestial navigation and dead reckoning. Columbus was known to be an expert in the latter.

Celestial Navigation

Celestial navigation is the science of determining one's geographic position by means of astronomical observations or, more specifically, by measuring altitudes of celestial objects - sun, moon, planets or stars in relationship to the horizon. Each star has a documented celestial latitude. If one knew the latitude of a star (how far north or south of the equator it stood), one could determine his position on Earth. If one wished to travel east across the Atlantic in a straight line, it was necessary to keep a star off the ship's starboard side at the same altitude from the horizon. If the altitude became greater between readings, it may have indicated that the ship was drifting south creating a greater angle between it and the star, which occurred at certain times of night. Likewise, if the measurement of the height of the star became smaller, one could conclude that he was drifting north, placing the star closer to the horizon in his view.

Deduced (Dead) Reckoning

The second technique was known as deduced reckoning or dead reckoning. This was Columbus' technology of choice for navigating. Dead reckoning (DR) is the process of determining your position based on a previously known position or a "fix". If you know your speed, direction and time traveled from a known position then you can determine your new position. The standard method of determining speed in the days of Columbus was to mark a line at the front of the ship and then place a second line at the back of the ship. A sailor stood at each line (which was a known distance) and the sailor at the front would drop a float into the water and start a chant. When the sailor at the rear of the ship saw the float, which was generally a fire log, pass his mark at the back of the ship, he would shout and the last word of the chant was noted. This chant provided a time of travel of the float between the front and rear marks. Because the distance between the two lines was known, and the medieval chant was used as a timer, the chanters knew the exact time of travel of the float and could therefore calculate the ship's speed for that day. This speed was assumed to be the average for the day and the distance traveled that day could be calculated. That distance would be measured out on the ships map from the last measurement, thus providing the current position of the ship. A compass or some form of direction certainty was necessary to accurately plot the line for the day's travel. Columbus used a standard compass to be certain he would maintain a westward path. When he made changes to the direction of his ship's travel the plotting of his deduced reckoning was adjusted to match his compass direction.

Columbus invented more accurate methods of dead reckoning. He would throw the float overboard with a rope tied to it. When he heard the float hit the water he started timing using an hourglass that had a known time to empty. This was more accurate than the chant method. Columbus tied a knot in his rope every 10 feet so he could simply count the knots that passed through his hand to determine the distance that the float had traveled. When the hour glass ran out he would stop counting and again calculate a distance that his ship had traveled. If 50 knots passed through his hand (each 10 feet apart) in the period of one minute, then 500 feet of rope had been released. Thus his ship was traveling at 500 feet per minute or (500 feet x 60 minutes) 30,000 feet per hour (or about 6 miles per hour). If he had traveled at this speed for a full day (24 hours) then his ship had traveled 720,000 feet that day; about 136 miles. Furthermore, Columbus learned that taking measurement several times a day would increase the accuracy of his dead reckoning maps.

[Author's note: It was during a workshop in Cleveland, Ohio, that an attorney asked if the term "knots" came from Columbus' technique. The term is still used today to measure the speed of ships and airplanes. After researching this term, the author confirms that theory. A "knot", equal to 1.15 miles per hour, came from the practice of observing a log tied to a knotted line to determine speed.]

Early Location Systems

Early location systems used a variety of tools:
Lighthouses: Provide a "fix" or location from which to determine your position.
Compasses: Provide a direction of travel for plotting distances traveled.
Landmarks: Provide a "fix" for navigation.
The Sun: Provide accurate determination of time or direction.
Maps: Provide distances through careful measuring and plotting of landmarks.
Early Techniques Were Subject to Dramatic Failures

Amelia Earhart

Techniques such as dead reckoning were not accurate by today's standards. In fact, a single misjudged measurement would lead to inaccurate navigation for the duration of a trip.

The most dramatic of the failures of location systems was the infamous death of Amelia Earhart in 1937. Using dead reckoning from her take off point in Lae, New Guinea she failed to find her destination Howland Island, located 2,556 miles from Lae in the mid-Pacific. Numerous times she back tracked to a known point and repeated the processes until she ran out of gas and crashed into the sea with her navigator. In *Naval History Magazine*, 2000, it was discovered that the location of Howland Island on her map was incorrectly placed. This was discovered through photographs of the aviator holding the map before her journey. Howland Island was actually 5.8 nautical miles from its charted position. The inaccurate map and no other form of navigation doomed her flight.

Compass Flaws

Although compasses were known to be accurate, many navigators soon discovered a flaw. If we think of the North Pole as True North we are correct; however a compass is driven (in simple terms) by the Earth's magnetic poles. The Magnetic North and South Poles differ from the geographic North and South Poles. Rather than running from the top of the Earth through to the bottom, the magnetic pole is angled through the earth starting at 11 degrees west of the North Pole and running through the earth to emerge 11 degrees west of the South Pole. As you move north to south traversing the magnetic pole, more drastic adjustments must be made to your compass to assure it reads accurately. This fact is known today and pilots adjust their compasses as a routine part of their take off checklist. You'll see that GPS devices automatically adjust for this effect through stored maps that define the degree of adjustments that must be taken.

There are two points where the magnetic poles meet the earth's surface and these points have the most dramatic effect on compasses, causing them to be inaccurate by as much as 10 to 20 degrees.

Magnetic North is in the North Atlantic near Prince of Wales Island, Alaska, while the South Pole, magnetically speaking, is found in an area of Antarctica, 1,500 miles from True South.

There also exists a path known as the Agonic Line where True North and Magnetic North are the same. Part of this line passes from Miami, Florida extending southeast to San Juan, Puerto Rico and northwest to Bermuda. Compass adjustments are unnecessary on this line, though traveling slightly east of this line to the Biminis Islands requires a 2 degree adjustment. As a navigator travels across this area, either east or west, some dramatic compass adjustments may be necessary. Within this oblong area, which many define as a triangle, many ships have lost their way or outright disappeared. Magnetic anomalies in this area may be one explanation for the strange and unexplained events of the area known as the Bermuda Triangle or as many conspiracy theorists call it, the Devil's Triangle. Rapid changes in weather, pirates, gas venting from the earth's core and the more colorful UFO theories are other explanations for ships that either disappear or are found completely abandoned yet intact in the Bermuda Triangle.

Even Christopher Columbus, the well respected navigator, made a note in his ship's log on the day before he discovered the new world, that his compass was suffering from deviations of as much as 11 degrees as he passed through this area. The next day, after passing successfully through the Bermuda Triangle, he discovered the New World.

More modern systems

There have been other types of position location systems developed, including Long Range Navigation (LORAN), angle of arrival (AOA), mobile telephone system positioning and inertial navigation system (INS).

While these systems cannot provide the accuracy or the ability to rapidly update location measurements, they are sometimes used with GPS systems as backup systems.

The reason that GPS is so successful today is that companies such as SiRF have built extremely small GPS chips that are highly sensitive radio receivers that can accomplish calculations extremely quickly. This allows for the continuous updating of location for high speed turn-by-turn directions and other applications.

GPS provides users with an accurate position on the Earth's surface. At best this position can be within inches of the true location. Today's GPS systems, when turned on, may take a few minutes to warm up but, when ready, they can take readings from four satellites almost instantaneously and complete the necessary computations to determine position in near real-time.

The GPS system continues to evolve. The next generation of GPS systems is adding new broadcast frequencies along with additional ranging codes to improve accuracy and reliability. The electronic chip that is the GPS receiver is so small that five of them can sit on your finger tip. With the addition of power, a clock source and an antenna, and a healthy set of satellites in orbit, the GPS system is ready to create even more accurate and rapid measurements of location for navigation, positioning and mapping devices.

Global Positioning System (GPS)

The global positioning system is a location determination network that uses satellites to act as reference points for the calculation of position information. These man-made reference points can be viewed as aerial lighthouses that are visible to user equipment and can also transmit additional information that can provide extremely accurate location information to the GPS function within location determination devices.

Several orbiting satellite systems are used for global positioning, which include:

United States Global Positioning System (GPS)
Russian Global Navigation Satellite System (GLONASS)
European Galileo System
Beidou Navigation Satellite System

The USA GPS System

The USA Global Positioning System (GPS) is a location determination system that was developed by the Department of Defense's (DOD) Ivan Getting, and Massachusetts Institute of Technology (MIT).

This system, which consisted of eleven satellites, was called NAVSTAR (Navigation System with Timing and Ranging) and launched between 1978 and 1985. By 1980, 18 satellites were part of the NAVSTAR constellation and used by the military for GPS.

In 1983, President Ronald Regan declassified GPS technology, allowing for public use. This was prompted by the take down of Korean Airline 007 by Russian Military jets when the commercial airliner drifted into Russian airspace. Since then, public use of the satellites for commercial purposes was allowed and by July of 1995, 24 satellites were in place, completing the full system. It was off-limits to the public between 1990 and 1993, during the first Gulf War, to allow for exclusive use by the military. Although the constellation currently has 31 satellites in orbit [1], only 24 are required for normal operation leaving 7 spares in case of lost operation.

GLONASS

The GLONASS system is a global positioning system that is operated by the Russian Republic, (State Unitary Enterprise of Applied Mechanics). The system has continued to evolve, providing more accuracy and precision, and much like the US system, it also has 24 satellites. Unlike the US satellites, which are launched individually, GLONASS satellites can be launched in groups of three. Additionally, the GLONASS system operates at a higher altitude than the US system. There are some technical trade offs to this approach such as better accuracy in the northern hemisphere at the cost of less accuracy in the southern hemisphere. Since GLONASS serves the Russian Republic, this is in their favor.

European Galileo System

The European Galileo System is a global navigation system similar to the US GPS system, which was started in May 2003 by the European Union and the European Space Agency. It is expected to be fully complete by 2020 and will have 30 satellites (27 operational + 3 active spares) [2] . Galileo is designed to provide more accurate horizontal and vertical position measurements at high altitudes and has two-way search an rescue communication capabilities allowing distressed users to have an indication that help has been requested [3]. China, Korea, Israel and other non-EU countries are invested in the project and will use the system as well.

Beidou Satellite Navigation System

The Beidou System is a Chinese regional satellite positioning system. It is a two-way satellite system that has been operating in a limited version since 2000 that allows mobile devices to request position information from the satellite network. The first experimental system (BeiDou-1) consists of 3 satellites that offer limited coverage. The second generation system COMPASS or BeiDou-2 (BDS) will have 35 satellites when fully completed. It is expected to offer global positioning services by 2020 [4].

Terrestrial and Other Positioning Systems

Terrestrial positioning systems are position location systems that use land-based transmitters to act as reference points for the calculation of position information. Some of the terrestrial based positioning systems include long range aid to navigation (LORAN), dead reckoning (DR), and inertial navigation systems (INS).

How GPS Works

Recall that there are 24 satellites being used in the US GPS system at all times. These satellites orbit the earth in such a way that at any given time and location, at least four satellites are visible to a GPS driven device. Each satellite is equipped with an extremely accurate atomic clock so the satellite is always aware of the current time on earth. The satellites are also aware of their own positions with the assistance of ground stations that give continuous updates. The 24 satellites orbit the earth transmitting their time and position. These pieces of data are received by the antennas attached to radio receivers inside a GPS device.

As a GPS device starts up, it must scan its radio tuner for very faint GPS satellite signals. Once it has collected data (the position of a satellite and the time the satellite sent the position) from at least three satellites, a location fix can be made.

Differential time of arrival and trilateration are the methods used to determine location in a GPS system. Dead reckoning may also be used when satellites are not visible.

Differential Time of Arrival

Differential time of arrival is the method used to determine how far each satellite is from a GPS device. Although each satellite transmits its position and the time it was at that position, it takes time for that signal to reach the earth. The receiver contains a very accurate clock, which can determine the difference in time between the current time and when the satellite sent the signal. With this differential time and the speed of radio waves, the distance from each of the three satellites can be determined using the simple formula -

Rate x Time = Distance

Trilateration

Trilateration is a method that is used to determine position on earth in three dimensions. GPS deals with three-dimensions rather than two. Since the distance from the earth to a satellite results in a sphere rather than a flat circle, the calculation is a bit complex.

Using trilateration, rather than drawing circles to determine position we need to draw spheres. For example, if the first acquired satellite is 11,000 miles from a position, one cannot simply draw a circle around that satellite and determine a position 11,000 miles from it. A sphere must be plotted, extending toward earth and away from earth. A second satellite is calculated to be 25,001 miles from position, resulting in another sphere. The two spheres intersect, creating a perfect circle. A circular plane now exists, extending down through the earth and out into space. A large number of potential positions have now been eliminated, but there is not yet an exact location. Many potential positions still exist and a third satellite is needed to define a sphere that intersects with the two current spheres, resulting in two points that define possible position. One point is in space and one is on earth. Since the world is roughly a sphere, the point in space can be eliminated and the approximate position of the GPS receiver is located on earth. A fourth satellite is necessary to account for altitude and provide an exact fix of the location. The plotting of a fourth sphere provides the exact location and altitude of the receiver at the time the four measurements were taken.

Figure 1.1 shows a global positioning satellite (GPS) system. This diagram shows how a GPS system receives and compares the signals from orbiting GPS satellites to determine its geographic position. Using the precise timing signal based on a very accurate clock, the GPS receiver compares the signals from three or four satellites. Each satellite transmits its exact location along with a timed reference signal. The GPS receiver can use these signals to determine its distance from each of the satellites. Once the position and distance of each satellite is known, the GPS receiver can calculate the posi-

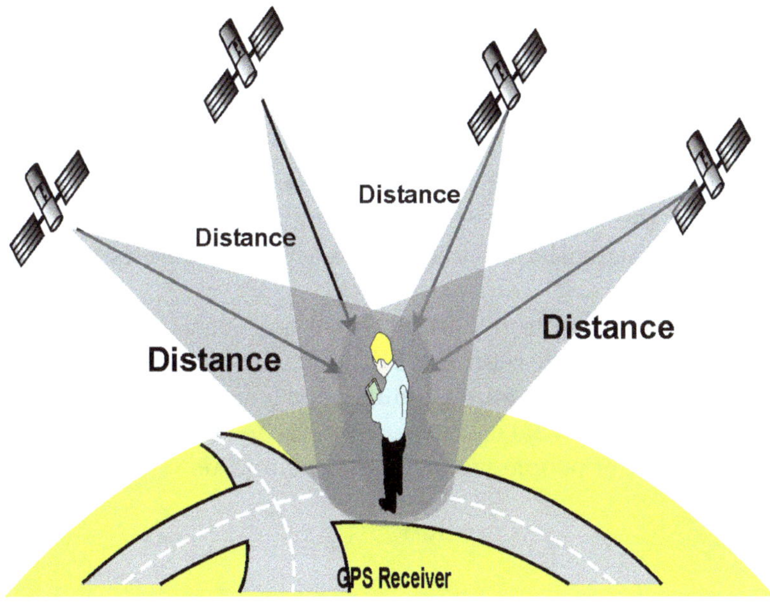

Figure 1.1, Global Positioning System (GPS)

tion where these distances cross. This is the location. This information can be displayed in latitude and longitude form or a computer device can use this information to display the position on a map on a computer display.

Computational Speed

Computational speed is the method used to determine the velocity, if any, of the GPS receiver in relation to the satellite(s), and is essential to accurate navigation. Position readings must be made once from each satellite from the same position on earth. Movement of the receiver will result in inaccurate readings. It is necessary to remain stationary and take four satellite readings or take the four readings almost simultaneously. Any other method will be inaccurate.

It is not necessary to take readings instantaneously if the receiver is stationary. Any amount of time can elapse after the location of the first satellite is received before the second satellite's location information is received as long as there has been no movement. The first satellite provided its position and moved on with its orbit and is no longer at the same position. This is irrelevant as long as all satellite readings are taken from a single position.

It is important to note that more than four satellites can be used if they are available and if the GPS device is programmed to take advantage of the additional data. This will yield even more accurate results.

Since GPS systems operate by simply receiving signals from satellites and there is no interaction between a GPS device and a satellite, an unlimited number of devices can be simultaneously served. Just like there is no limit to the number of people who can listen to a radio station, in GPS there is no limit to the number of people who can receive and use GPS satellite signals.

Detailed Technical Information

Each GPS satellite transmits two frequencies; 1575.42 MHz (the L1 carrier) and 1227.6 MHz (the L2 carrier). A GPS receiver compares the signals from multiple GPS satellites (4 satellite signals previously mentioned) to calculate the geographic position. This allows the GPS system to provide very precise vehicle or device locations. The GPS system is composed of three segments; the user segment, the space segment and the control segment.

User Segment

The user segment is the portion of a communication system which interfaces the system to users. For the global positioning system, the user segment includes the receivers and the interface support systems (such as assisted data) they interact with. Since the GPS system broadcasts information that does not require responses from receivers, it can serve an unlimited number of users.

Space Segment

The space segment is the portion of a satellite system that is composed of the satellites, their power systems, navigation systems, and communication equipment. Satellites transmit one or more signals (downlink) to the earth and receive control and other processing information from ground control systems. For GPS systems, the uplink signals contain information about the precise time the message is sent, the position of the satellite and atmospheric information that can be used to correct changes in signal propagation (time delays) that can affect the accuracy of position location calculations.

Control Segment

The control segment (CS) is the portion of a communication system that coordinates the operation of its key components. The CS in a global positioning system (GPS) monitors and controls the position and operation of the transmitted signals from the satellites. The GPS control segment includes a master control station (MCS) that can transfer the satellite (uplink) position control and satellite position data to the satellites. The MCS also receives GPS satellite position information from monitor stations. The GPS system has several monitoring stations located around the world that gather information about the location of GPS satellites and send it back to the MCS.

Figure 1.2 shows that a GPS system contains three key segments; user segment, space segment and control segment. The user segment receives the signals from four or more satellites to calculate its position. The satellite segment creates time related and satellite position messages and transmits them on two frequencies to the user devices. The satellite segment also receives an uplink control and position data from the ground segment. The ground segment controls the position of the satellite above the earth as it rotates and sends ground position reference information to the satellite.

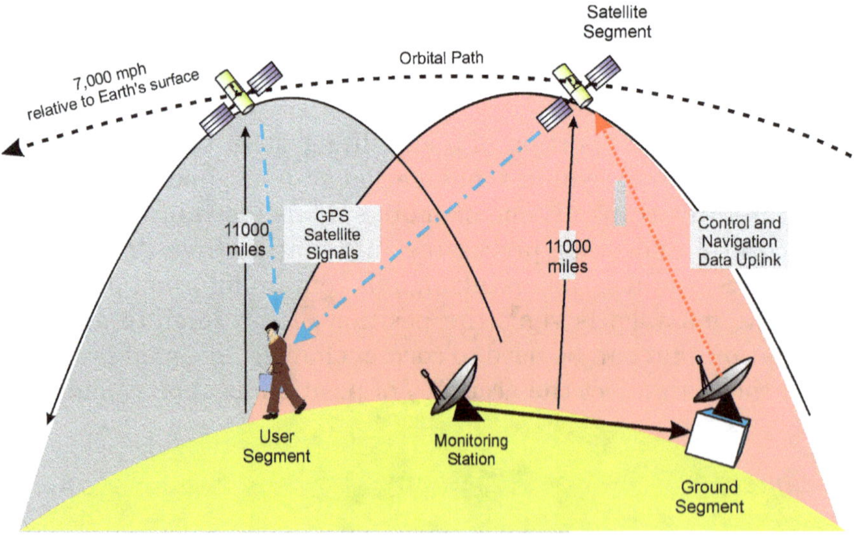

Figure 1.2 Global Positioning System Segments

GPS Signal Availability

GPS signal availability is the ability to detect, receive and decode a transmitted signal so that some or all of the information carried can be extracted or used. GPS signal availability is influenced by satellite visibility and satellite health.

Satellite Visibility

Satellite visibility is the ability of a receiver to sense or receive a signal from a satellite. GPS radio coverage is a geographic area that receives a GPS radio signal above a specified minimum level. A GPS receiver typically requires a clear radio channel to at least four satellites. If there are more than four visible satellites, the receiver may be able to determine which ones will provide the most accurate signals (satellite geometry) or it may be able to use more than four GPS signals to improve its position accuracy.

GPS satellites are medium earth orbit (MEO) satellites that move at approximately 7,000 miles per hour relative to the surface of the earth. This means that satellite visibility will be lost as the satellite moves over the horizon and new satellites will become visible as they approach the horizon.

GPS satellites are divided into groups that rotate the surface of the earth in six patterns (orbital planes). This constellation helps to ensure that from most locations on earth, at least four GPS satellites will be visible at any time.

Satellite Health

Satellite health is a set of characteristics, including performance characteristics such as timing accuracy, which define the ability of a satellite to perform its designed function. When a GPS satellite cannot provide a signal it is called a satellite outage.

Satellite outages are periods of time during which satellite signals are unavailable. Satellite outages may be caused by a variety of factors including equipment maintenance, equipment failure and sunspots.

GPS System Operation

GPS systems operate by finding and acquiring signals from GPS satellites, measuring the propagation time from the satellites and calculating the position relative to the known locations of satellites.

Satellite Constellation

Satellite constellation is the arrangement of space vehicles (satellites) around the planet. Groups of GPS satellites rotate the earth sharing an orbital path (orbital plane). An orbital plane is the flat reference area that contains all the points where a satellite or other object can move in its orbital rotation. The GPS system has six orbital planes.

Satellite Acquisition

Satellite acquisition is the process of adjusting a ground receiver unit so that its antenna and receiver can receive and demodulate the signal from a satellite.

During the signal acquisition process, the GPS receiver searches GPS frequencies until it can detect a signal. It then locks onto the signal and acquires the basic information about the GPS satellite that is transmitting the signal. The GPS receiver may then use this information to receive and decode additional codes that are transmitted by that satellite.

Satellite Almanac

A satellite almanac is a composition of data related to the estimated position and status of satellites over a period of time. While the satellite almanac has relatively low accuracy, it can be used to determine the expected location of satellites to enable a more rapid signal acquisition process.

Satellite Tracking

Satellite tracking is the process of measuring and processing information received from a satellite to determine the location and/or characteristics of the signal from the satellite. Once a satellite signal is acquired, the receiver will be adjusted to allow it to track the satellite as it moves (GPS satellites move at approximately 7,000 mph above the earth).

Propagation Time Measurement

Propagation time is the period that is required for a signal to travel between points on a transmission path. By determining the propagation time and knowing the radio signal propagation speed, the distance from the GPS satellite can be calculated with confidence due to the extremely accurate time clocks. Determining the initial distance from the satellite is called pseudo-ranging.

To determine the propagation time, the clocks in the GPS satellite and the GPS receiver are time synchronized. When the code from the satellite is transmitted, it is coded with the GPS time. When it is received in the GPS receiver, it is compared to the synchronized GPS time in the receiver. The difference between these times is the propagation time.

The GPS satellite transmits several types of codes. Some codes are available for any receiver to use (civilian codes) and others (more accurate and robust codes) are protected by encryption keys (military codes).

Figure 1.3 shows how propagation time from a satellite is calculated in a GPS system. This diagram shows that a GPS satellite sends a unique coded message at a specific time. The GPS receiver continuously looks for the unique satellite code and when it matches, it notes the time difference between when the message was sent and its internal clock. This difference in time is the propagation time.

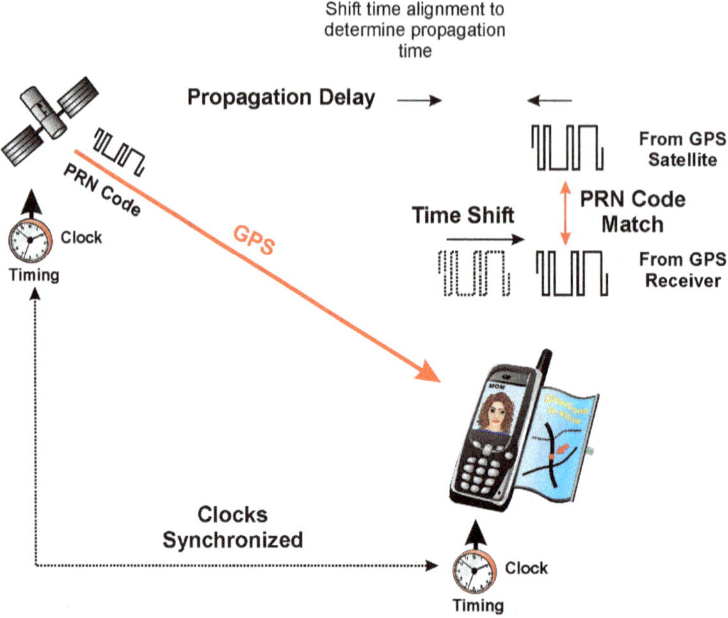

Figure 1.3, GPS Carrier Propagation Time Measurement

Carrier Phase Measurement

Carrier phase measurement is the comparison of the phase crossings on a received signal or relative signals. GPS carrier phase measurement is the process of counting the number of received signal cycle crossings between code signal matches. Knowledge of the frequency (period of each cycle) allows the number of cycle crossings to be converted into a time measurement.

Broadcast Ephemeris

Broadcast ephemeris is the transmission of a table of astronomical information that provides the location of many celestial bodies (such as satellites) at specific time intervals. GPS satellites periodically transmit their satellite position information in a navigation message. The position information is used in combination with the distance calculation to determine the position of the GPS receiver.

Distance Calculation

Distance calculation is the process of determining the distance between a GPS receiver and a satellite. Distance calculation involves determining the propagation time and adjusting for variations (delays) that occur, which can distort the distance calculation.

The first step in distance calculation is determining the amount of time it takes a radio signal to travel from the satellites to the receiver. The speed of light is the velocity that light waves travel. In vacuum (similar to air), the wave speed of a light wave is about 300 million meters per second (186,281.6 miles per second). In other materials, the speed that light waves travel is lower. By knowing the amount of time signals take to travel between the GPS satellite and the GPS receiver, and the speed the radio signal travels, the approximate distance can be calculated. A simple rule of thumb for distance calculation is that a radio signal will travel approximately 1 foot (30 cm) in approximately 1 nanosecond.

The GPS system uses different types of codes that offer different levels of accuracy and signal robustness. The GPS system offers standard positioning service (SPS) and precise positioning service (PPS).

Standard Positioning Service (SPS)

Standard positioning service is a GPS service that provides basic information that can be used to determine position location. SPS provides location information through the use of a C/A-code.

Precise Positioning Service (PPS)

Precise positioning service is a GPS service that provides enhanced information that can be used to more accurately determine position location. PPS provides additional information through the use of a P-code.

Receiver Initialization

Receiver initialization is the process of capturing initial parameters that are used by the communication system. For GPS systems, receiver initialization can be used to gather and correct some of the errors created by the GPS system.

Receiver initialization involves the process of setting up a GPS receiver at a known location. When the GPS signal is captured, the position error offset is stored. The GPS receiver is then moved to a nearby unknown location. The offset values from the initialized location can be applied to the new location to increase the accuracy of the location information.

Figure 1.4 shows how receiver initialization may be used to correct some of the biases and errors in the GPS system. This diagram shows that a GPS receiver is initialized at a known location. The received GPS correction values can be updated and stored using the known location information. When the GPS receiver is moved to a nearby position, the updated correction parameters can be used to improve the accuracy of the measurements.

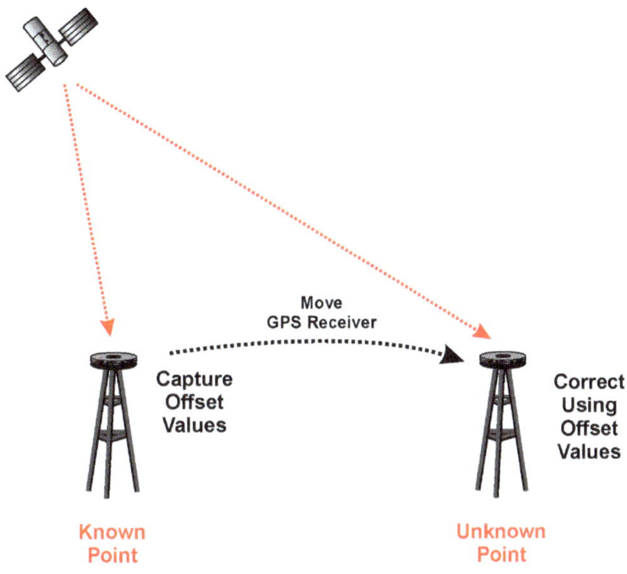

Figure 1.4, GPS Receiver Initialization

Relative Positioning

Relative positioning is the process of improving the accuracy of positioning systems (such as the GPS system) through the use of multiple (relative) location receivers that are tracking the same location signals. Relative positioning uses position information from a known base location, which is transmitted to another remote (rover) GPS receiver device.

GPS Base Station

A GPS base station is a receiver that collects GPS data, which it transfers to remote locations. The GPS base station may be at a fixed location so it can adjust received data to correct for errors and/or biases received from the GPS satellite signals.

Rover Station

A rover is a receiver (such as a GPS receiver) that collects data at remote locations. The rover's position may be recorded or computed relative to another reference source (such as a fixed GPS receiver).

Figure 1.5 shows how relative positioning can be used to increase the accuracy of a GPS position measurement. This example shows a receiver at a known position (the base) and another receiver at an unknown position (the rover) for relative positioning. This diagram shows that because the GPS position errors between the base and the rover are approximately the same, the difference between the known and unknown locations can be used to improve the accuracy of the position measurement.

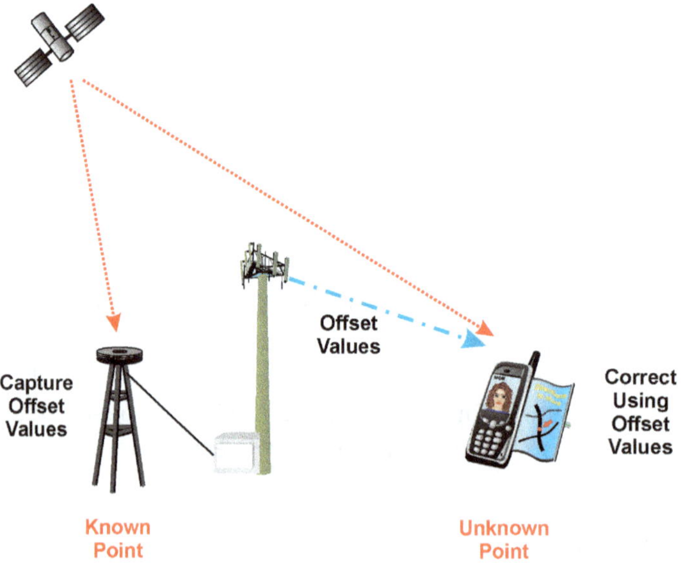

Figure 1.5, GPS Relative Positioning

Real Time Kinematic GPS (RTK GPS)

Real time kinematic GPS is a position location process whereby signals received from a reference device (such as a GPS receiver) can be compared using carrier phase corrections transmitted from a reference station to the user's roving receiver. Using the correction information, RTK systems can provide real time accuracy below 5 cm.

Figure 1.6 shows how the RTK GPS system uses a base GPS receiver to gather and transfer information to a GPS rover receiver. The data from the base receiver can be used by the roaming receiver to calculate more accurate position information in real time (or near real time).

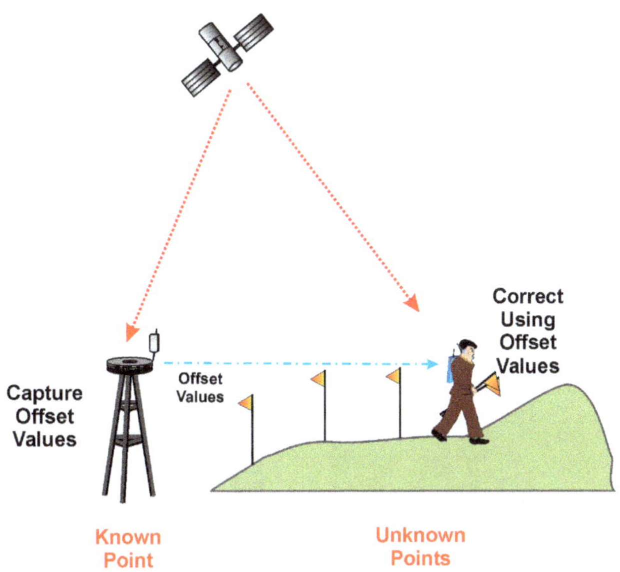

Figure 1.6, GPS RTK Operation

GPS Base Repeaters

GPS base repeaters are devices or circuits that are located between a GPS satellite and a GPS receiver that can refocus or improve the quality of the signal that is delivered between them. A GPS base repeater receives the data from the base GPS receivers and retransmits it to the roving GPS receiver. These may be used in construction sites or areas that have limited line of sight capability.

A repeater station is a fixed radio transceiver that performs automatic retransmission of radio communications that are received from one or more stations and directed to a specified receiver site.

Figure 1.7 shows how a base repeater can be used to extend GPS base signals into areas that may not have direct communication paths to GPS base receiver signals. This example shows how the received data from the base GPS receiver is relayed through another transmitter to the roving GPS receiver.

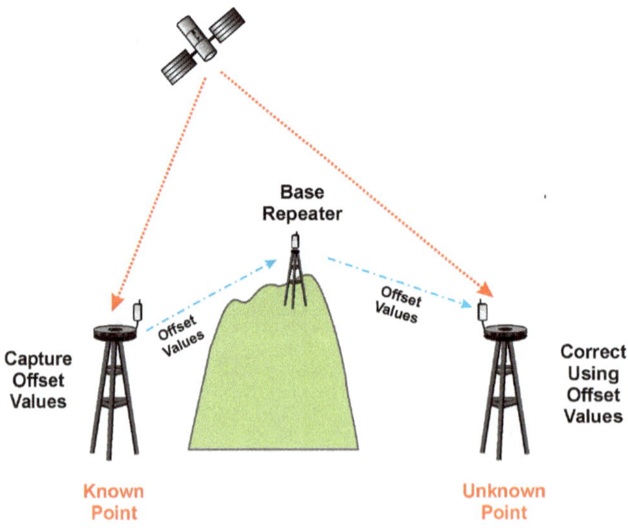

Figure 1.7, GPS Base Repeaters

Differential Global Positioning Service (D-GPS)

Differential GPS is an enhancement to the GPS system that uses a network of radio beacons to create a fixed grid of known reference points in order to improve the accuracy of the GPS signal.

A reference station is a receiver that is located at a stationary or fixed point that has a known location. A reference station may be used to gather or provide information that can be used by other receivers (such as GPS satellites) to correct errors and/or biases.

Post Processing

Post processing is the performing of operations or calculations on information or data after the event that created the information or data has occurred. To perform post processing, the GPS receiver stores its information in a data file (data logging). The data log is then updated with an observation file to provide more accurate position information.

A data logger (also called a data recorder) is a data storage device that can store measurement data over a period of time (such as from a GPS receiver). An observation file is a collection of data that represents the measurements (observations) of a device or system (such as GPS satellite position and related information parameters).

Figure 1.8 shows how the GPS system can use post processing to improve the accuracy of position information. This diagram shows that the initial position measurements are calculated using estimated satellite position data. This diagram also displays that the GPS tracking stations can provide more accurate position information after the GPS information was captured. The more precise GPS satellite location can be used to determine more accurate position measurements.

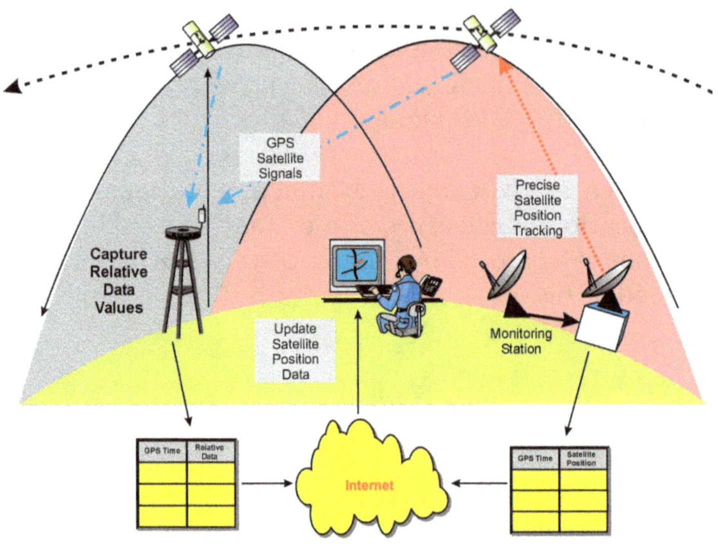

Figure 1.8, GPS Post Processing System

Post Processed Kinematic (PPK)

Post processed kinematic is a GPS position location process whereby signals received from a mobile location receiving device store position data that can be adjusted using corrections from a reference station after the data has been collected. Using PPK, very high accuracy can be achieved.

GPS Receiver

A GPS receiver is a device that can receive, decode and process GPS satellite signals and the results of the processing can be displayed or sent (interfaced) to other devices. GPS receivers may be capable of static and/or dynamic position measurements.

Static positioning is the process of gathering location information while the user or location-receiving device is at the same relative position as its reference points. Static positioning may take advantage of recording position information over extended time periods allowing for the averaging of biases and errors.

Dynamic positioning is the process of gathering location information while the user or location-receiving device is in motion. Some GPS receivers with limited processing capability may not be able to perform dynamic positioning due to the rapid changes in the received signal or the inability to track the GPS satellites.

Single Frequency GPS Receiver

A single frequency receiver is a device or signal capturing system that can select and receive signals on a single frequency channel during a specific time period. Single frequency receivers are generally less expensive and less accurate than dual or multiple frequency receivers.

Dual Frequency Receiver

A dual frequency receiver is a device or signal capturing system that can select and simultaneously receive signals on two frequency channels during a specific time period. A dual frequency code receiver is a device or signal capturing system that can select and simultaneously receive coded signals on two frequency channels during a specific time period. Dual frequency receivers generally have higher accuracy than carrier phase receivers.

GPS Interfaces

GPS devices may interface to other devices or accessories (such as display assemblies). Interfacing capability is the ability of a device or system to connect and/or communicate with other devices or systems.

To operate with other devices or accessories, GPS receivers may include electrical or wireless interfaces. Wireless interfaces such as Bluetooth can be used to link satellite receivers to displays at nearby locations (such as linking the GPS receiver in the trunk to a display device on a car dashboard).

GPS interfaces may be used to import or export data. Import data can include correction signals that adjust GPS measurements for varying conditions such as adjusting the radio transmission time as a result of changes in ionosphere electron count levels. GPS interfaces may also be used to capture data (data logging) from the device to allow for post processing.

Manufacturers including Trimble and Garmin have defined protocols that can be sent over standard serial busses to setup, configure, transfer data, and control GPS receiver operation.

Assisted GPS

Assisted GPS (A-GPS) is any position location technology that uses another location information system or source (such as radio signals from mobile telephone systems) to enhance the accuracy and/or reliability of the global positioning system (GPS). Assistance can be in the form of acquisition (helping to find and initialize receiver) or computational (processing location information).

Acquisition Assistance

Acquisition assistance is the process of adding information to assist in the finding, tracking or processing of acquired signals. This can significantly speed up the receiver time.

Computational Assistance

Computational assistance is the process of using information to assist in the calculation or processing of information. This can increase the accuracy of the receiver information while reducing the complexity (processing capabilities) of the receiver.

Some mobile telephone systems have been enhanced to provide GPS satellite information to GPS enabled devices to assist them in acquiring satellites. The mobile base station can transmit the known base station position information to mobile GPS receivers to allow them to find and acquire satellites more quickly. Helping mobile telephones to quickly find GPS satellites is called a "warm start."

GPS Satellites

A satellite is a telecommunication device that is placed in space. A satellite vehicle (SV) is an object containing communication electronics that revolves around another object of greater mass (such as the earth). The force of attraction (gravity) of the larger object determines the satellite's motion. Satellites contain power systems, attitude (position) control systems, and communication equipment.

GPS satellites are a combination of receivers and transmitters (transponders) that receive signals from earth stations (uplink) and retransmit them to GPS receiving stations (downlink). They are located at 17,700 km (approximately 11,000 miles) above the surface of the earth and travel at approximately 7,000 kilometers per hour.

Each GPS satellite transmits two frequencies with 20 to 50 Watts of RF power. GPS satellites are assigned space vehicle numbers by which they are uniquely identified. The satellites transmit unique reference codes.

The design life (life span) is the operational time during which a device or system is expected to operate. For satellite systems, a key design life limitation is the amount of propulsion fuel that is used to keep the satellite in its desired orbital plane. Most of the satellite attitude propulsion fuel is used to initially position the satellite into its desired orbit.

The life span of GPS satellites has increased from 4.5 years on the original Block I satellites to more than 11 years on the new Block IIR satellites.

The weight of GPS satellites ranges from approximately 1,800 pounds (900 kilograms) to over 4,400 pounds (2,200 kilograms). Their wingspan ranges from approximately 17 feet (5.3 meters) to 116 feet (35.5 meters).

GPS satellites contain computer processors, programs and memory areas. The processor is responsible for creating the navigational messages that are transmitted to GPS receivers. The first GPS satellites had limited memory and processing capability so they could only hold approximately 3.5 days of navigation message information. GPS satellites (Block II) can hold 180 days of navigation information.

In 2000, the US Congress authorized the creation of the GPS Block III Satellites that add new signals to enable a Distress Alerting Satellite System (DASS) and enhanced crosslink communication [[5]].

Power System

A satellite power system is a system that is used to supply energy to the communication and computing equipment within a satellite. GPS satellites receive their power from solar energy. The satellite stores excess energy in batteries so it can operate when the solar panels are not facing the sun. The GPS satellite must continuously reposition its solar cells towards the sun as it orbits around the earth. The amount of power that solar cells can provide ranges from approximately 800 Watts for Block II GPS satellites to more than 2,450 Watts for Block IIF GPS satellites.

Attitude Control System (ACS)

An attitude control system is a system that maintains the position and orientation of satellites. Attitude control systems in satellites use a combination of momentum wheels, magnetic coils and thrusters to adjust the satellite's position.

A momentum wheel is a device that controls the force applied to an object (such as a satellite) by changing the velocity and direction of a spinning wheel.

Magnetic coils are windings of wires that can create magnetic fields. A magnetic coil may be used to develop a small force that can be used to adjust (fine tune) the position of an object (such as adjusting the position or direction of a satellite).

Thrusters are mechanical jet assemblies that redirect fluids or gasses to produce a force that can be used to change the position of a satellite. Because thrusters use chemicals that are kept in limited supply on satellites, the attitude control system will attempt to use the momentum wheel and magnetic coils before using the thrusters.

Sending commands from the control segment to the satellite performs attitude control. Newer versions of GPS satellites have autonomous navigation (Autonav) capability. Autonav is the ability of a device or object to automatically track and adjust its own position.

Communication Equipment

GPS satellite communication equipment is the devices used to send and receive messages between satellites and GPS systems and can include receivers, transmitters, timing references (clocks), and optical reflectors.

Receivers

GPS satellite receivers convert RF signals into control and data signals that are used by the satellite. Control signals include attitude (position) control and program instructions (for satellites that can have their programs updated).

Transmitters

GPS satellite transmitters convert satellite position data (ephemeris) into navigation messages that are periodically transmitted on two frequencies (L1, L2). Block IIF satellites have the capability to transmit three frequencies (L1, L2 and L5).

Satellite Clocks

Satellite clocks are reference timing signals that are used to decode and synchronize information from assemblies and communication links. Because timing is critical for determining position, GPS satellites use highly precise atomic clocks. An atomic clock is a reference timing signal generator that uses the atomic properties of a molecule (such as Cesium or Rubidium) to create the reference timing signal.

Optical Reflectors

Optical reflectors are objects that redirect (reflect) light signals. Newer GPS satellites include optical reflectors that allow Laser signals to be reflected which are used for precise distance measurement (cm accuracy).

Figure 1.9 shows the functional components of a GPS satellite. This diagram shows that the GPS satellite contains power, an attitude control system and communication equipment. The power system is composed of solar cells and a battery storage system. The attitude control system contains chemicals and a flywheel (momentum) to control the position (attitude) of the satellite. The communication system contains a receiver, a transmitter and a precise time reference clock.

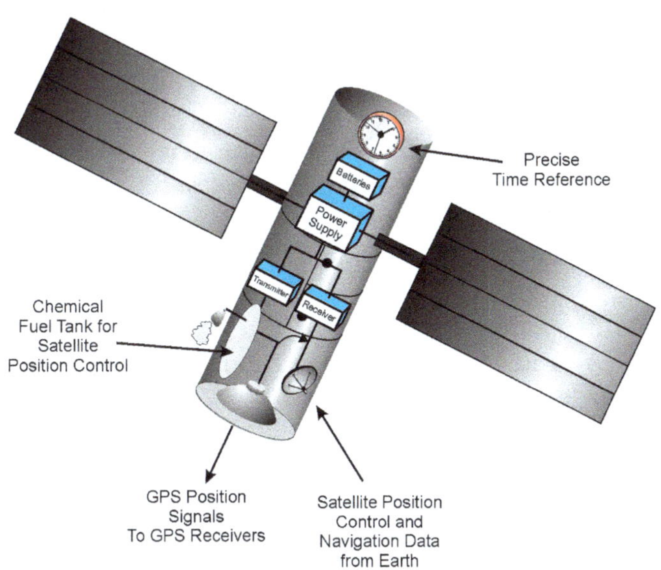

Figure 1.9, GPS Satellite Operation

Block I Satellites

Block I satellites were the original GPS space vehicles, which were no longer in service as of 1995. The original design lifetime of the satellites was 5 years but some of the Block I satellites provided service for 10 years. Block I satellites could operate without uplink navigational data for 3.5 days.

Block II and IIA Satellites

Block II satellites were the 2nd generation of GPS satellites which were designed to have a 7.5 year operational life span. Block II satellite improvements included radiation hardened electronics assemblies, 180 day navigational message storage capability, and more robust and secure message delivery.

The radiation hardening protects electronic assemblies from component damage and changes to signals (such as stored memory elements) due to radiated energy signals (such as solar radiation). Radiation hardening increases the reliability (improved satellite health) of GPS satellites.

Extended navigational message storage capacity allows for the satellite to continue providing service even when the uplink is lost. While the loss of uplink control will result in changes in the satellite's orbit, it will still be able to provide some useful information for up to 180 days.

Block II satellites added the capability to increase accuracy using selective availability (SA) and to provide more robust code signals for anti-spoofing operation.

Block IIR Satellites

Block IIR satellites are an improved version of Block II GPS satellites. They have lower cost than Block II satellites and a 10 year design life span.Block IIR satellite improvements included the ability of the satellite to determine its own position (Autonav), improved accuracy and reprogrammable uses processors.

Block IIR satellites included autonomous navigation ability, which eliminated the need for navigational control messages from the earth. The GPS satellite could use inter-satellite ranging to determine position. Block IIR satellites had data processors that could be updated (reprogrammed).

Block IIF Satellites

Block IIF satellites are the GPS satellites that replaced Block IIR satellites. Block IIF satellites transmit a high power third GPS frequency (L5), have a much larger and more powerful solar array and transmit signals for civilian users. Block IIF satellites have an 11 year life span design.

Block III Satellites

Block III satellites will replace IIR satellites providing all existing signal capabilities and adding new Distress Alerting Satellite System (DASS) service, enhanced crosslink communication, and Laser positioning control. Block III satellites provide all Block IIF signals plus a new L1C civil signal. Block III satellites are expected to become operational by 2017 and have a 15 year lifespan [6].

Figure 1.10 shows the different types of GPS satellites and their capabilities. Block I satellites had basic GPS navigation capability, lasted up to 10 years and ended service in 1995. Block II satellites had a longer design life,

Satellite Group	Key Features	Notes
Block I	Design Life 5 Years Stores Navigation Messages up to 3.5 Days	Lasted up to 10 Years Ended service in 1995
Block II	Design Life 7.5 Years Stores Navigation Messages up to 180 Days Anti-Spoofing (AS)	Radiation Hardened to Improve Reliability
Block IIR	Self Navigation (Autonav) Reprogrammable Processors	Lower Cost than Block II Design Life of 10 Years
Block IIF	Adds L5 Frequency Large Solar Array New Civilian Code	Design Life 11 Years

Figure 1.10, GPS Satellite Types

improved radiation hardening and could process navigation messages for 180 days. Block IIR satellites had automatic navigation (autonav) capability along with reprogrammable processors. Block IIF satellites can transmit on a new frequency (L5), have a much more powerful solar array and transmit more robust civilian codes on three frequencies (L1, L2 and L5).

GPS Satellite Orbits

A satellite orbit is the path of a satellite or other object in space relative to a specified frame of reference, as described by its center of mass when subjected solely to natural forces (mainly gravitational attraction).

The orbit of a satellite is determined by orbital mechanics. Orbital mechanics is the science that is used to understand, determine and estimate the orbit of a satellite. Orbital mechanics can be described by Kepler's Laws of Planetary Motion.

Kepler's Laws of Planetary Motion are a set of rules defined by the scientist Kepler about the orbits of planets around the sun that include elliptical orbits, equal time intervals and orbital time periods. Kepler's Laws can be applied to the orbit of man made satellites around the earth.

Kepler's First Law of Planetary Motion

Kepler's First Law of Planetary Motion is a rule that states that the orbital paths of the planets (satellites) are elliptical with the sun (focal point) at one focus of the ellipse.

For satellites that orbit the earth, the orbital point with the largest distance from the center of the earth is called the Apogee. This distance can be used to calculate the worst case transmission loss and delay time. The Perigee point is the orbital point of a satellite that is at a minimum distance from the center of the earth.

Figure 1.11 shows Kepler's First Law applied to earth's orbital path. This diagram shows that an orbital path has an elliptical shape where it revolves around a focal point (such as the sun). The closest point from the sun's focal point of the orbital path is called the Perihelion point and the point furthest away from the sun's focal point is called the Aphelion point.

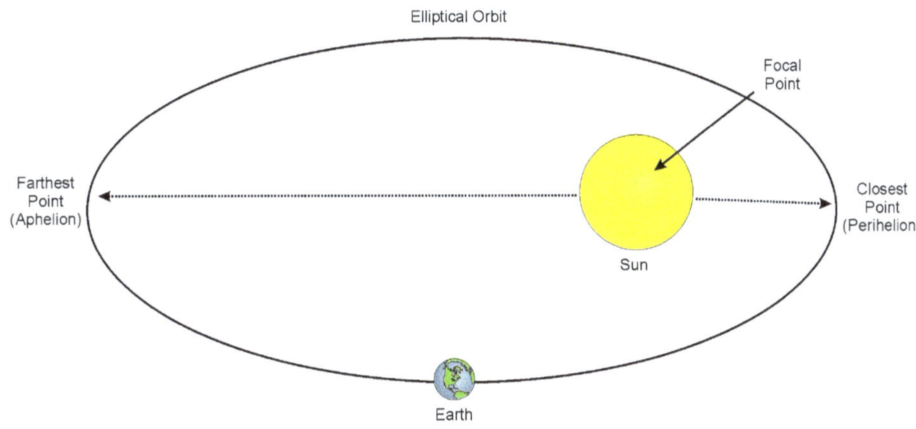

Figure 1.11, Satellite Orbital Path

Kepler's Second Law of Planetary Motion

Kepler's Second Law of Planetary Motion is the rule that the lines joining the planet (the satellite) to the sun (the focal point) sweep out equal area in equal time as the planet travels around the ellipse (orbital path).

Figure 1.12 shows Kepler's Second Law applied to satellite orbital path. This diagram shows that the orbital time periods are related to area covered by the satellite with reference to the focal point. This example shows that the satellite moves faster in areas of satellite orbit that are close to the focal point and slower at points that are located farther away from the focal point.

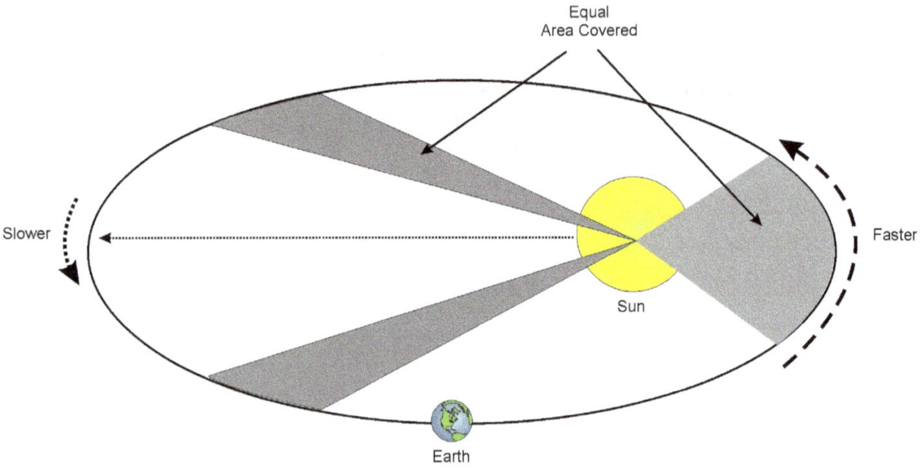

Figure 1.12, Satellite Orbital Travel Speed

Kepler's Third Law of Planetary Motion

Kepler's Third Law of Planetary Motion is the rule that states that the orbital period is proportional to the cubes of the semi-major axes. Kepler's Third Law can be used to determine the orbital time period.

The orbital period for a GPS satellite is approximately 11 hours and 58 minutes. The GPS orbital time period is commonly referenced to be 12 sidereal (solar) hours. Sidereal solar time adjusts our time for changes in the solar system.

Satellite Perturbing Forces

Satellite perturbing forces are external influences (changes) on the orbital path of a satellite around an object. Some of the perturbing forces on satellites include gravitational fields from the sun and other planets, fluctuations in the earth's gravitational field, solar radiation, and atmospheric drag.

Gravitational fields from other celestial bodies are perturbing forces are called third body effects. As the satellite moves around the earth, its orbital path is modified by the gravitational forces from moons and planets (such as the earth's moon and the sun).

The satellite orbit is also changed by fluctuations in the earth's gravitational field. These variations occur due to tide changes and variations in the surface and shape of the earth.

Solar radiation is the transferring of energy from the sun (such as in the form of photons) onto another object. Solar radiation can influence the position of a satellite as a result of the photons hitting the satellite (radiation pressure) when traveling from the sun and reflecting off the surface of the earth. There is also an upward solar pressure effect from the light that is reflected from the earth, called the Albedo Effect, to the satellite.

Atmospheric drag is a force that is imposed on an object (such as an airplane or satellite) as it moves through the atmosphere. Because GPS satellites are located well above the atmosphere of the earth, the atmospheric drag force is negligible.

Figure 1.13 shows how external forces may alter satellite orbits. This diagram shows how a satellite experiences external influences from gravitational forces from the sun and the moon. The satellite also experiences forces from photons that hit the satellite from the sun and photons that hit the satellite as they are reflected off the earth. This example also shows that variations of the earth's gravitational field influence the satellite's orbit, as well.

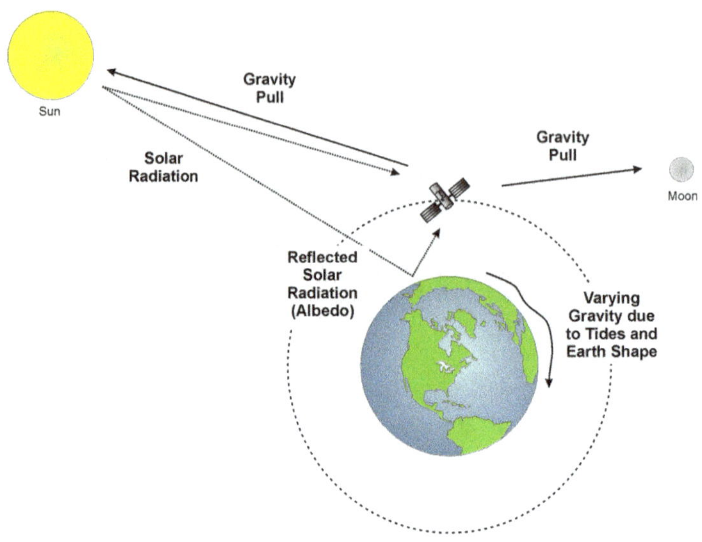

Figure 1.13, Satellite Perturbing Forces

GPS Pseudolites

GPS pseudolites are transmitters that provide signals that mimic the signals that would have been transmitted by satellites. Pseudolites may be used to provide global positioning signals to GPS receivers in areas that are unable to receive signals (such as mining pits) from enough GPS satellites to determine their position.

Pseudolites may be used to provide GPS signals to locations that have limited satellite visibility such as cities with tall buildings or mining pits. To provide a GPS receiver with enough satellite reference signals so it can calculate its position (four satellites needed), a pseudolite creates a new GPS reference signal.

Using GPS pseudolites can result in a near-far radio problem. The near-far problem occurs during the reception of radio signals where the signal strength of one or more simultaneous signals (such as coded signals on the same frequency) becomes too strong or too weak as the receiver moves closer to or further away from one or more of the transmitter sources. If the GPS receiver gets close to the pseudolite, the signal may be so strong that the GPS receiver cannot demodulate or decode the GPS satellite signals.

Figure 1.14 shows how a GPS pseudolite can be used to provide GPS service in areas which may have obstructed views of GPS satellites. This diagram shows that the GPS pseudolite operates as one of the GPS satellites that the GPS receiver uses to gather its position information. This diagram shows that the GPS receiver is not capable of obtaining four satellites without the use of the pseudolite because of the surrounding terrain.

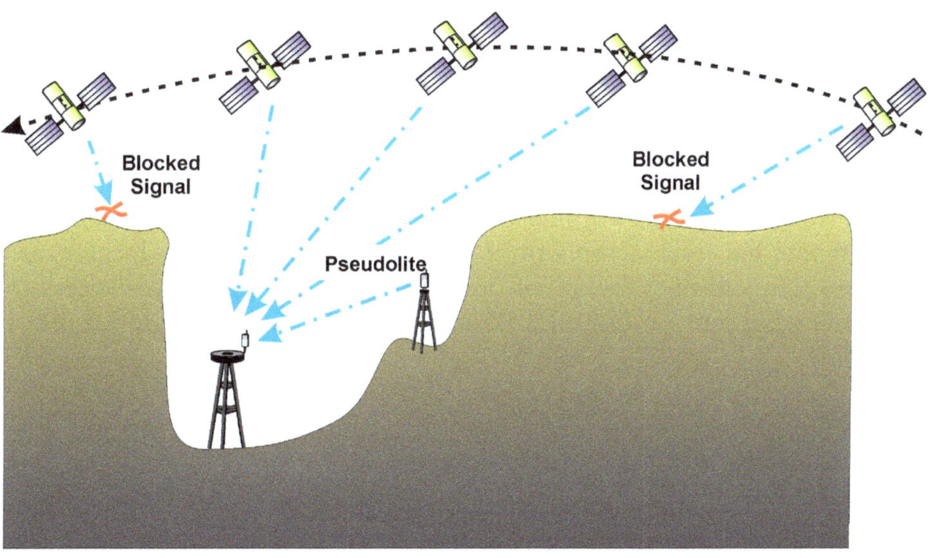

Figure 1.14, GPS Pseudolite Operation

GPS Operational Control Segment (GPSOCS)

The operational control segment is the communications gateway and the system that communicates and controls satellites. The control segment in global positioning systems monitors and controls the position and operation of the transmitted signals from the satellites. The GPS operational control segment (OCS) is composed of a master control station (MCS) and monitor stations.

Master Control Station (MCS)

A master control station is the primary controlling system that is used in a satellite communication network. The master control station uploads orbital and clock data to space vehicles (SVs) which use the uploaded information to create navigation messages and other data that are broadcast from the satellites to GPS receivers. The GPS master ground station is located at Falcon Air Force Base in Colorado Springs, Colorado. Because controlling GPS satellites is important, the GPS system has a backup master control station (BUMCS) that is located in Gaithersburg, MD.

Monitor Stations

Monitor stations gather signals from SVs, which are used to calculate the orbital model for each of the satellites. Monitor stations are located around the world (Hawaii and Kwajalein in the Pacific Ocean; Diego Garcia in the India Ocean; Ascension Island in the Atlantic Ocean; and Colorado Springs, Colorado).

GPS Radio Signal Characteristics

GPS radio signal characteristics are the elements that make up the received signal and can include frequency, modulation, power level and channel coding.

Frequency

A frequency band is the difference between the upper and lower frequency boundaries that is defined for a specific type of radio service. GPS transmitters label the transmitted frequencies L1, L2 and L5 (Block III satellites).

L1 Carrier

The L1 carrier is a transmission frequency for a global positioning system (GPS) satellite that is 1,575.42 MHz.

L2 Carrier

The L2 carrier is a transmission frequency for a global positioning system (GPS) satellite that is 1,227.60 MHz.

L5 Carrier

The L5 carrier is a transmission frequency for a global positioning system (GPS) satellite that is 1,176.45 MHz.

Pseudo-Random Noise (PRN) Codes

A pseudorandom noise code is a unique identifier that is used by a transmitter (such as a GPS satellite) to modify or encode a signal. Each GPS satellite can transmit any one of several different types of codes and each code is unique for that satellite.

Clear Acquisition Code (C/A Code)

The clear acquisition code is a position reference code provided by the global positioning system for the standard positioning service. The C/A code is a sequence of 1,023 pseudo-random binary biphase modulations on the GPS carrier and it is sent at a chip rate of 1,023 MHz. The C/A code is also known as civilian code.

The C/A code contains a handover word (HOW), which can be used to help find the P code. The HOW is a message containing synchronization information that assists in the transfer of tracking from a C/A code to a P code.

L2 Civil Long (L2 CL)

L2 civil long is a long length ranging code used for civilian applications that are sent on the L2 carrier channels of a GPS satellite.

L2 Civil Moderate (L2 CM)

L2 civil moderate is a medium length ranging code used for civilian applications that are sent on the L2 carrier channels of a GPS satellite.

Precise Code (P Code)

A precise code is a long sequence of pseudo-random binary biphase modulations sent by a GPS satellite which provides enhanced accuracy and is used by the military. The P-code is sent at a chip rate of 10.23 MHz that repeats about every 267 days.

Anti-Spoofing Code (Y-Code)

The Y-code is an encrypted version of the ranging P-code that is sent on the global positioning system (GPS). The Y code can provide anti spoofing protection.

Anti-spoofing (AS) is a process that adds encoding protection to a reference signal to ensure others cannot jam or modify the underlying information. AS is used on the global positioning system (GPS) to encrypt (scramble) the P-Code so non-authorized users cannot obtain a higher level of accuracy offered by the GPS system.

A W-code is a key that is used to encrypt a P-code to produce a Y-code that is sent by a GPS satellite to allow decode capability only to those receivers that have the W-code. This encryption process helps to ensure the ranging codes received by the military have not been altered.

Military Code (M-Code)

The M-code is an encrypted GPS ranging code that is used on the global positioning system (GPS) for military purposes. The M-code has better jamming resistance than the Y-code.

GPS Time

GPS time is a reference timing signal that is used to time tag GPS signals. GPS time is a continuous clock signal that was set to UTC on January 6th, 1980. GPS devices and systems use or reference GPS system time and coordinated universal time.

GPS System Time

GPS system time is a timing signal that is provided by atomic clocks that are located in the GPS ground control stations. GPS time started at zero at midnight on January 6th, 1980. Since the GPS time clock was started, it has only been changed by leap seconds. As a result, the GPS system time was ahead of UTC in 2006 by 14 seconds.

Coordinated Universal Time (UTC)

Coordinated universal time is a reference time scale that is maintained by the Bureau International de l'Heure (BIR). UTC is commonly used as the basis of coordinated dissemination of standard frequencies and time signals used in communication systems.

Universal Time 1 (UT1)

Universal time 1 is a reference time scale that adds leap seconds to the time UTC value maintained by the Bureau International de l'Heure (BIR). UT1 adjusts time for small changes in the earth's rotation.

International Atomic Time (TAI)

International atomic time is a time scale that was developed by the Bureau International de l'Heure. TAI is based on reference timing signals that are provided from atomic clocks operating in several locations that conform to the International System of Units.

GPS Data Formats

GPS data formats are the positional and semantic structures that are used to separate information items (records) from the elements (fields). Various groups and companies have created a variety of ASCII (text based) and binary data format structures that can be used to store and transfer GPS information.

GPS data formats can be used to store, transfer and retrieve position location and correction. Post mission is the processing or usage of information after a mission (such as measuring location information) has been performed. GPS precise satellite ephemeris data may be provided for post mission processing through other types of data connections such as the Internet.

Receiver Independent Exchange Format (RINEX)

Receiver independent exchange format is an industry standard text based data format used to exchange GPS data between GPS receivers and systems. The RINEX format includes GPS and GLONASS observation data, navigation messages, clock data and SBAS broadcast data files. RINEX is overseen by the international GNSS services (IGS) agency.

Compact Receiver Independent Exchange Format (CRINEX)

Compact receiver independent exchange format is the compressed (optimized) version of the industry standard text based data format used to exchange GPS data between GPS receivers and systems.

Standard Product 3 (SP3)

Standard product 3 is an industry standard format for precise GPS orbital (ephemeris) data. SP3 is overseen by the International GNSS Services (IGS) Agency.

Ionospheric Map Exchange Format (IONEX)

Ionospheric map exchange format is a standard data structure that defines the total electron count (TEC) in the ionosphere.

Radio Technical Commission for Maritime Service (RTCM)

The Radio Technical Commission for Maritime Service is an advisory organization that oversees the SC-104 industry standard format for transferring global positioning differential position signals data between GPS devices and stations. More information about RTCM can be found at www.RTCM.org.

National Electrical Manufacturer's Association 0183 (NEMA-0183)

The National Electrical Manufacturer's Association industry standard 0183 is a standardized electrical interface that enables marine electronic devices to communicate with each other. The NEMA-0183 standard transfers ASCII data and is capable of a variety of command and data transfers including GPS data.

Figure 1.15 shows some types of GPS data formats. These formats include RINEX data in text format which can exchange data information between the GPS system and GPS receivers and the compressed RINEX (CRINEX) format. GPS satellite orbital data can be transferred in standard product 3 format. Ionosphere total electron count (TEC) levels are transferred in IONEX format. The radio technical commission for maritime service has defined GPS error correct data format in standard SC-104. Electrical interfaces for GPS devices can use the National Electrical Manufacturer's Association standard 0183 (NEMA-0183) format.

Format	Purpose
Receiver Independent Exchange Format (RINEX)	Exchange format for GPS data between GPS receivers and systems
Compact Receiver Independent Exchange Format (CRINEX)	Compressed version of RINEX
Standard Product 3 (SP3)	Standard format for precise GPS orbital (ephemeris) data
Ionospheric Map Exchange Format (IONEX)	Map data for Ionosphere total electron count.
Radio Technical Commission for Maritime Service (RTCM) SC-104	Standard error correction data format for maritime users.
National Electrical Manufacturer's Association (NEMA) NEMA-0183	Standardized electrical interface for devices.

Figure 1.15, GPS Data Formats

GPS Errors

GPS errors are unwanted variations in position measurements that come from a variety of sources. Without corrections to the errors, the location accuracy of the GPS system is within approximately 50 to 100 meters. GPS errors include propagation errors that can result from changes in atmospheric conditions, inaccurate satellite position data (ephemeris), reference timing errors (clock drift), multipath transmission and selective availability.

Atmospheric Conditions

The atmosphere is composed of materials or elements that surround the earth. The earth's atmosphere can be divided into layers that have different effects on the propagation of radio signals.

Atmospheric conditions define the characteristics of the atmospheric regions. Atmospheric layers are regions separated by height above the surface of the earth, which contain gases and materials with common characteristics. Atmospheric layers include the troposphere (directly above the earth to 12 km), the mesosphere (12 km to 50 km), the stratosphere (50 km to 90 km), and the ionosphere (90 km to 400 km).

Atmospheric data is information that identifies the characteristics of the atmosphere. Atmospheric data may be used to define how objects (such as satellites and radio signals) will interact with and be changed by the earth's atmosphere.

Radio propagation is the process of a radio signal (electromagnetic signal) traveling from one point to one or more alternate points. Radio propagation may involve a direct wave (space wave) or a wave that travels along the surface (a surface wave). Radio propagation characteristics typically vary based on the medium of transmission (air) and the frequency of radio transmission.

Troposphere

The troposphere is a layer of the earth's atmosphere, between the surface and the stratosphere, in which about 80 percent of the total mass of atmospheric air is concentrated and in which the temperature normally decreases with altitude.

The ionosphere and troposphere both refract GPS signals. This causes the speed of a GPS signal in the ionosphere and troposphere to be different from the speed of a GPS signal in space. Therefore, the distance calculated from the formula: signal speed x time, will be different for the portion of the GPS signal path that passes through the ionosphere and troposphere and for the portion that passes through space.

Stratosphere

The stratosphere is the atmospheric layer that lies between the troposphere and the mesosphere, which is approximately 50 km to 90 km above the surface of the earth.

Mesosphere

The mesosphere is the atmospheric layer that is located between the stratosphere and the ionosphere, and is approximately located between 12km to 50 km above the surface of the earth.

Figure 1.16 shows the different layers of atmosphere above the earth. The troposphere is the first layer that extends up to approximately 12 km. It is followed by the mesosphere layer that ranges from 12 km to 50 km. The stratosphere layer is located from 50 km to 90 km and the ionosphere ranges from 90 km to over 400 km.

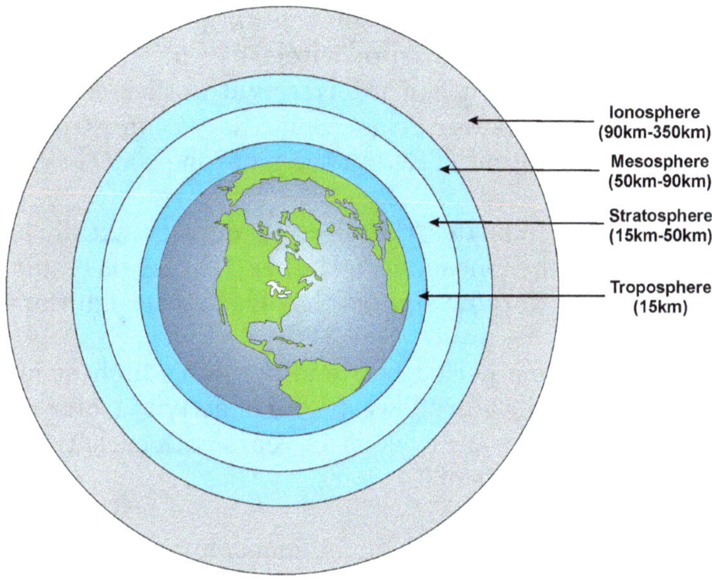

Figure 1.16, Atmosphere Layers

Ionospheric Delay

Ionospheric delay is the amount of additional transmission time a signal incurs as it passes through the ionosphere. The amount of delay through the ionosphere varies with the electron density and frequency of the signal that is passing through. The electron density can vary based on solar flare activity.

Ionospheric delay can be compensated or adjusted by using an ionospheric model. An ionospheric model is a mathematical representation of the transmission characteristics of a signal as it passes through the ionosphere and can be used to compensate for ionospheric disturbances. An ionospheric disturbance is a rapid increase in the ionization level in the ionosphere. Ionospheric disturbances can be caused by solar flares and this can result in increased radio wave signal level absorption.

A solar flare is an explosion that occurs on the sun. Solar flares generate a significant amount of energy that can contain photons and photonic particles. Solar flare activity can disrupt wireless communication. If solar flare activity is strong enough, it can interfere with other electromagnetic systems (such as electrical power grids). Solar flares can result in an increase in the total electron content (TEC) in the ionosphere.

TEC is a value that indicates the electron density within an area of the atmosphere (such as the ionosphere). Higher TEC levels result in increasing delays and distortion to radio signals that travel through the area.

A solar cycle is the time period between the sun's highest level of activity (solar maximum) and the sun's lowest level of activity (solar minimum). The average time period of a solar cycle is 11 years with cycle time ranging from a low of 9 years to upwards of 14 years.

The transmission delays caused in the ionosphere affect GPS transmitted frequencies differently. L2 (the lower frequency) is delayed (bent) more than L1 (the higher frequency).

Figure 1.17 shows how ionospheric delay can effect the transmission of GPS radio signals. This example shows that the amount of ionospheric delay varies based on the electron density and that the electron density can vary based on geographic location and sunspot activity. This diagram also shows that the amount of delay is different for the different GPS frequencies.

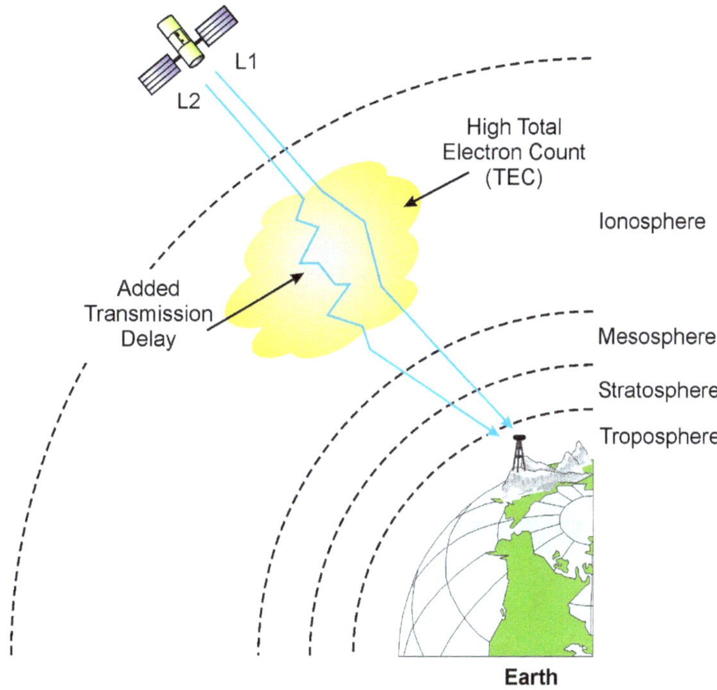

Figure 1.17, GPS Satellite Ionospheric Delay

Ephemeris Errors

Ephemeris errors are differences in the identified and actual position data of the satellite. Ephemeris information is periodically broadcast from the satellite. In 2007, the accuracy of GPS broadcast ephemeris data was approximately 1.6 meters.

More accurate satellite position data can be obtained from monitoring stations (GPS tracking) after the GPS receiver has taken its measurements. This data can be used to update (adjust) the measured data to provide more accurate position locations.

Timing Errors

Timing errors are differences between when a signal occurs and when it is expected or anticipated to occur. GPS timing errors include satellite clock drift and receiver clock offset.

Clock Drift

Clock drift is the amount of change in a reference timing characteristic that occurs over a period of time. Clock drift can be used to adjust and correct measurements that are time based. For example, in GPS systems, the distance from a GPS satellite to a GPS receiver is calculated using timing signals that are referenced to the satellite clock. Changes in the reference timing result in position inaccuracy so clock drift offset values can be used to increase the position accuracy. In GPS systems, clock drift information is contained within the broadcast ephemeris (orbital position) information.

Receiver Clock Offset

Receiver clock offset is a value that is used to adjust receiver clock time. Receiver clock offset may be used to adjust the clock for periodic time changes that were not applied to the receiver clock (such as GPS clocks).

Multipath

GPS multipath is the propagation of a radio signal that can travel through multiple paths such that part of the signal energy is received from one path before another part of the signal is received on another path that has been delayed. GPS multipath delay is due to the extra travel time for the other part of the radio signal that may have been reflected from a building, water region or mountain.

Multipath effect is the distortion in measurement or information accuracy that results from multipath signals.

The direct path to the receiver typically has the shortest transmission time. Earliest time period code match (correlation peak) can be used. Multiple paths that are received at the GPS receiver typically cause signal dispersion. The multipath effect can be reduced or eliminated through the use of directional antennas or through receiver design that can sense and subtract multipath signals.

Figure 1.18 shows how multipath effect can affect the measurement accuracy of a GPS system. This example shows that the transmitted signal energy from the GPS satellite can be directly received, but a portion of the energy may be received after it has been reflected by another object (such as

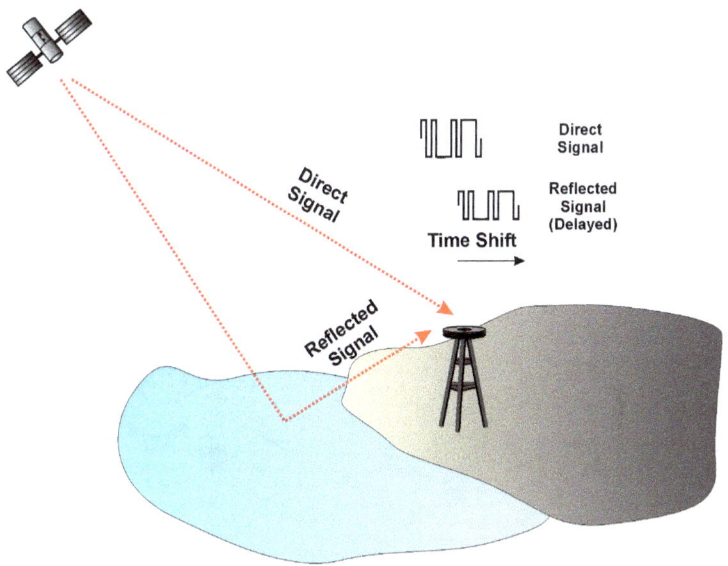

Figure 1.18, GPS Multipath Effect

water). This diagram shows that the multipath signal is delayed and it may have smaller signal energy level.

Satellite Geometry

GPS satellite geometry is the method that is used to determine the location of satellites (geometric position) when information is gathered. The satellite geometry effect is the influence on the accuracy or measurement values from satellites that varies with the geographic location of the satellites. In general, the further apart the satellites are, the higher the position accuracy they can provide.

Figure 1.19 shows how GPS satellite geometry can influence the accuracy of GPS position measurements. This diagram shows that when the satellite geometry is relatively close together, the accuracy is lower and when the satellite geometry has the satellites widely separated, the accuracy is better.

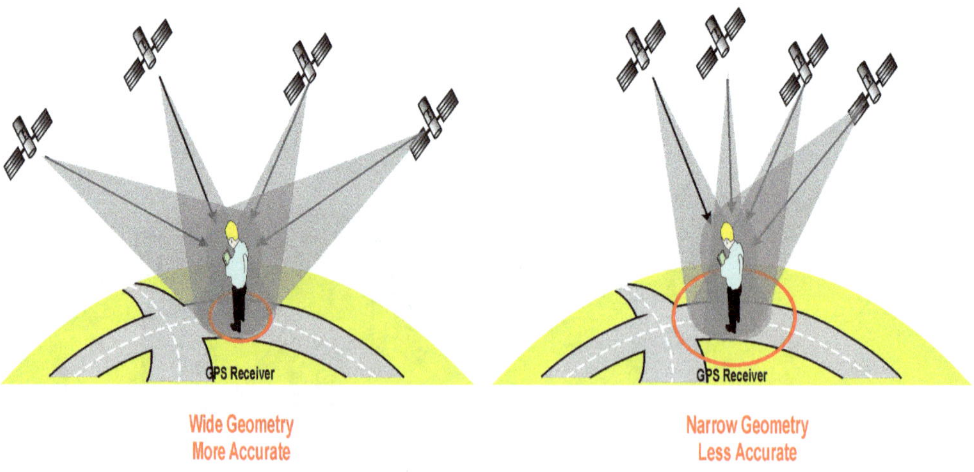

Figure 1.19, GPS Satellite Geometry

Dilution of Precision (DOP)

Dilution of precision is the inaccuracy of position determination that is caused by the use of reference satellites, which are located too close to each other. Higher values of dilution of precision indicate that the position measurement is less accurate.

Time Dilution of Precision (TDOP)

Time dilution of precision is the position inaccuracy that results from the relative time accuracy of its reference sources (GPS satellites).

Vertical Dilution of Precision (VDOP)

Vertical dilution of precision is the position inaccuracy that results from the relative vertical position of a device to the position and accuracy of its reference sources (GPS satellites).

Horizontal Dilution of Precision (HDOP)

Horizontal dilution of precision is the position inaccuracy that results from the relative horizontal position of a device to the position and accuracy of its reference sources (GPS satellites).

Position Dilution of Precision (PDOP)

Position dilution of precision is the inaccuracy that results from the relative horizontal and vertical position of a device to the position and accuracy of its reference sources (GPS satellites).

Geometric Dilution of Precision (GDOP)

Geometric dilution of precision is the position inaccuracy of position determination that is caused by the position and timing accuracy of its reference sources (GPS satellites). GDOP is the combination of time dilution (TDOP) and position dilution (PDOP).

It may be possible to program a GPS receiver to select a set of reference satellites that have a low DOP (wide geographic mix of reference satellites) to improve the accuracy of position measurements.

Figure 1.20 shows some of the causes of position errors in the GPS system. Atmospheric conditions in the ionosphere and troposphere slow down and redirect (refract) GPS radio signals. The orbital position information (ephemeris) and the timing of the GPS clock (drift) may be slightly off. The satellite information may be intentionally offset by the Department of Defense for security purposes. The GPS radio signals may be reflected off of nearby terrain such as mountains or tall buildings.

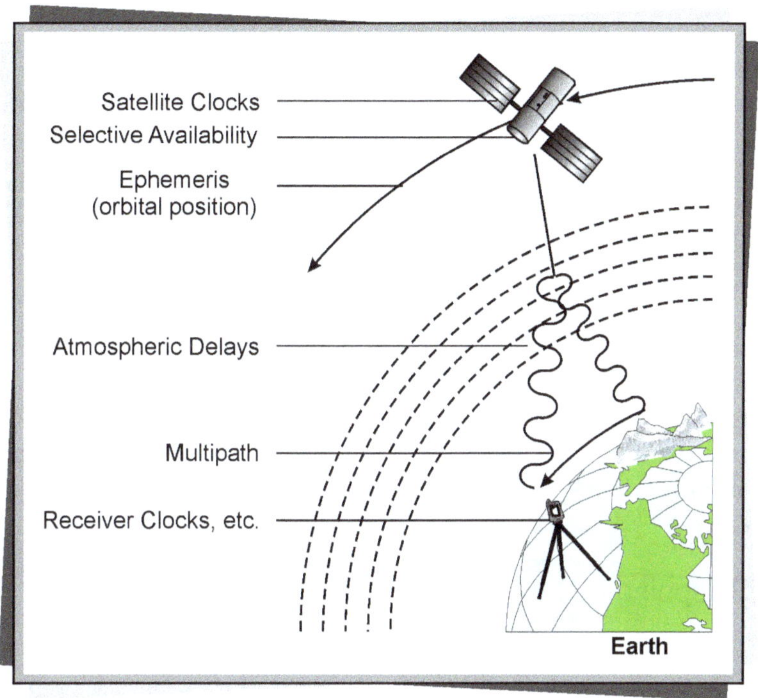

Figure 1.20, GPS Error Sources

Pseudo Range Corrections (PRC)

Pseudo range corrections are factors that adjust for the signal delays that occur when GPS signals are sent through the atmosphere.

Residual Errors

Residual errors are the net sum of the errors in a system or process, or the amount of inaccuracy of a position measurement that remains after all of the other errors have been adjusted.

Triple Difference GPS

Triple difference GPS is the process of taking the difference between measurements from two GPS receivers to reduce the GPS errors and biases. The GPS receivers simultaneously track the same satellites and measurements are taken over multiple intervals.

Selective Availability (SA)

Selective availability is the modification of timing information of GPS systems to intentionally cause inaccuracy. The intention of selective availability is to provide information to allow the military to correct and use very accurate position information while providing useful but not precise location information for commercial applications. SA introduces location errors of up to 70 meters.

Antenna Swapping

Antenna swapping is the process of making measurements with two receivers and swapping antennas (or swapping the receivers) so the measurement errors can be reduced. The antenna swap method may use one of the receiver's locations that is already known to normalize the measurements.

Antenna Offset

Antenna offset is the difference between the phase center point and the physical center point of an antenna.

Figure 1.21 shows how antenna swapping can be used to enhance the accuracy of GPS position measurements. This diagram shows that the antenna of the base receiver is swapped with the antenna of the rover unit.

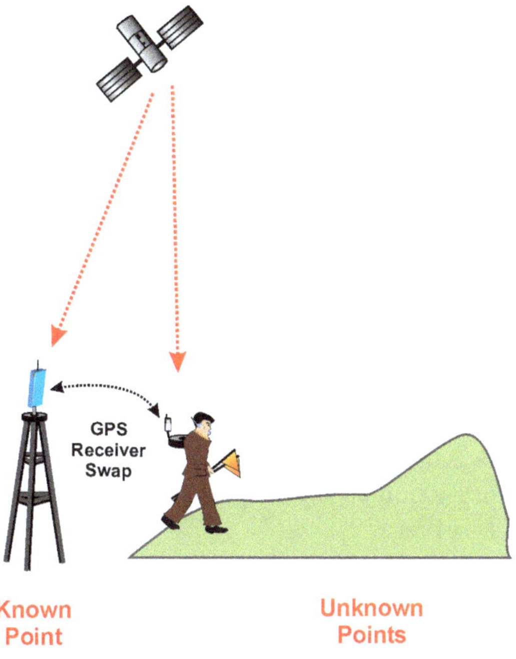

Figure 1.21, GPS Antenna Swap

Augmentation Systems

Augmentation systems are a combination of equipment and services that can provide information or capabilities to other systems to improve accuracy and performance. GPS augmentation systems provide additional information that can be used by GPS receivers to adjust or improve the accuracy of their measurements.

Augmentation systems gather GPS satellite and atmospheric information at various locations. This information is combined, processed and retransmitted to user devices. The user devices can use this information to adjust their measurements to improve the accuracy of the position information. Various GPS augmentation systems are located throughout the world.

Wide Area Augmentation System (WAAS)

The Wide Area Augmentation System is a network that provides additional information to augment information gathered and calculated by the GPS system. The WAAS provides a satellite signal for WAAS users to assist the routing and approach vectors for aircraft navigation. The Federal Aviation Administration provides funding for WAAS.

WAAS Reference Station (WRS)

A WAAS reference station is a fixed point GPS receiver point that has a known location which is used to gather GPS information that can be supplied to the Wide Area Augmentation System (WAAS). The WAAS gathers and processes the information so it can provide correct information to other GPS and GLONASS receivers.

European Geostationary Navigation Overlay System (EGNOS)

The European Geostationary Navigation Overlay System is a wide area augmentation system that provides additional information to augment information gathered and calculated by the GPS and GLONASS systems.

International GNSS Services (IGS)

International GNSS Services is a group of more than 200 worldwide agencies that voluntarily provide GPS & GLONASS station data to generate information that assists in increasing the accuracy of GPS & GLONASS measurements. IGS information can be found at http://igscb.jpl.nasa.gov.

GPS and GEO Augmented Navigation System (GAGAN)

GPS and GEO Augmented Navigation System is a wide area augmentation system in India that provides additional data to augment information gathered and calculated by the GPS system.

Enhanced Location Method

Enhanced location method is any position location technology that uses another position location information source (such as radio signals from a GPS or mobile telephone system) to enhance the accuracy and/or reliability of the provided position location information.

Wide Area Differential GPS (WADGPS)

Wide area differential GPS is a real-time differential GPS data source. The WADGPS system provides GPS signal correction information from a set of ground reference stations.

Long Range Aid to Navigation (LORAN)

Long range aid to navigation is a radio positioning system that provides location information by using the time difference between receptions of radio signals from two or more high power fixed transmitters.

The LORAN system uses a master transmitter and secondary transmitters. The secondary transmitters emit their timing pulses (time of emission – TOE) at fixed times after the master transmitter sends its timing pulses. By knowing the position of the transmitters and relative time that it takes for each of the signals to be received, a line of position arc can be mapped for each transmitter.

Line of position (LOP) is a sequence of points that represent the solution to the timing function from the transmitter time of emission. The LOP is determined by measuring the amount of time that has elapsed (time delay) for the reception of a pulse transmission. The LORAN receiver is located at the point where the LOP arcs cross.

The transmission of these timing pulses is repeated. Group repetition interval (GRI) is the time duration of a sequence of signals or pulses. GRI is used in the LORAN system to hold a sequence of timing pulses that include master and secondary pulses.

Figure 1.22 shows the basic components and operation of the LORAN system. This diagram shows that a LORAN system is composed of master and secondary transmitters that operate at approximately 100 kHz. The secondary transmitters are synchronized to the master transmitter and as each transmitter sends a sequence of pulses in succession, they are spaced in time so they do not overlap each other. This diagram shows that the receiver calculates the time difference between each pulse sequence to determine

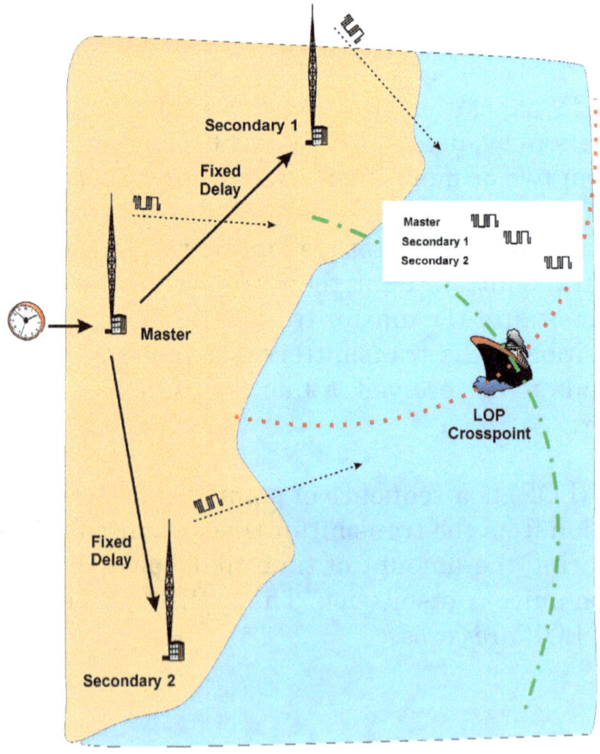

Figure 1.22, LORAN Navigation System

the distance from each transmitter to create a hyperbolic line of position (LOP). The location is at the point where the LOPs intersect each other.

Differential Long Range Navigation (Differential LORAN)

Differential long range navigation is an enhancement to the LORAN system that uses a LORAN reference transmitter station to provide a set of correction factors in order to improve the accuracy of the LORAN position calculation.

Enhanced Long Range Navigation (eLORAN)

Enhanced long range navigation is a version of the LORAN surface based navigation system that synchronizes the transmitter station to the same time of emission (TOE) reference.

Dead Reckoning

Dead reckoning is the process of determining a current location by using position change information in reference to a previously known location. The calculations may be based on speed, elapsed time and direction. Because the measurements used for dead reckoning have limited accuracy and the errors in position accumulate over time, precise navigation data is more likely to be obtained by other position location systems such as GPS or LORAN. Dead reckoning is more commonly used to update position location information during times and in areas where other position location systems are unavailable (such as when a GPS receiver is located in a tunnel).

Inertial Navigation System (INS)

An inertial navigation system is an assembly that is used to determine position location information that is calculated from the movement of the INS.

An INS contains an inertial measurement unit (IMU) along with computing systems that can process the acceleration (via an accelerometer), orientation and rotational information gathered from the IMU to provide relative position information. The INS calculates its position relative to a reference starting point. While the accuracy of an INS degrades with increases of distance from its initialization reference point, the INS is immune to jamming so it may be used as backup for other navigation systems such as GPS and LORAN.

Accelerometer

An accelerometer is a device or assembly that can measure the rate of change in velocity (acceleration) of an object.

Gyroscope

A gyroscope is a device that uses a spinning wheel on an axle to determine the orientation and angular momentum of an object. The gyroscope measures changes in the orientation of the spinning wheel (gyroscopic inertia) to determine if the acceleration and direction of motion tend to resist changes to their orientations due to the angular momentum of the wheel.

Vibration Gyroscope

A vibration gyroscope is a device that measures the changes in vibration of a material to determine the orientation and angular momentum of an object. When the vibration gyroscope moves, the Coriolis acceleration effect on the material produces a voltage that is proportional to the acceleration of the object.

GPS Applications

GPS applications are systems or devices that use positioning information to provide specific services or benefits to the user. Some key GPS applications include mapping, location monitoring, agriculture control navigation, navigation warfare (NAVWAR), surveying and structural deformation monitoring.

Because the GPS system has higher accuracy and much faster position updating than any other location system, it can be used to enhance or enable new applications. For example, continuously measuring position allows GPS receivers to determine velocity.

Mapping

Mapping is the process of gathering position information so that the locations and possibly the attributes of the items (roads or towers) can be presented in a form that can be interpreted by a user.

Utility Maps

Utility maps are graphic displays of the types of utilities that are located in a specific geographic area. Utility maps may combine several layers, and can be composed of location and terrain details of rivers, trees, land contours and roads. Additionally, other maps may be combined with utility facilities to produce utility maps.

Geographical Information System (GIS)

Geographical Information System is a data processing system that is capable of gathering, analyzing and providing geographic information. GIS is used to create maps or display the results of queries for the locations of objects or systems.

GPS can be used with other position ranging systems to gather data for a geographical information system. GPS signals may provide the primary location information, while secondary position information is gathered from other systems, such as sonar or laser ranging systems.

Airborne Mapping

Airborne mapping is the process of gathering location information via aircraft (land height, roads or towers) so that it can be presented in a form (a map) that can be interpreted by a user. Airborne mapping can be used to produce topographical maps. Topographical maps are graphic images that provide information on the elevation points of terrain and objects in a defined geographic area.

Seafloor Mapping

Seafloor mapping is the process of gathering seafloor location information (usually via ships with echo sounding sonar) so that it can be presented in a form (a navigation map) that can be interpreted by a user.

GPS and sonar can be combined to perform seafloor mapping. The GPS signals are used to determine the location of a ship, which is combined with sound navigation and ranging (sonar) information to create a seafloor map. Sonar determines the distance and direction of objects through the transmission and reflection (echo) of acoustic energy.

Three Dimensional Mapping

Three dimensional mapping is the process of gathering location information so that the locations and possibly the attributes of items (roads or towers) can be presented in a form that has three dimensions (latitude, longitude and height above sea level), which can be interpreted by a user. To perform three dimensional mapping, GPS systems may be combined with photogrammetry or laser ranging devices.

Photogrammetry is a process through which terrain elevation data can be accumulated with the use of a stereo image or 3D photograph. The two (or more) images captured via photogrammetry (similar to the viewpoint of human eyes) are compared to determine the distance from the camera, producing a 3D map.

Laser Range Finding

Laser range finding (LRF) is the process of estimating the distance or propagation time between a laser transmitter and an optical receiver. LRF devices can operate by sending a light pulse towards an object and measuring the amount of time it takes the pulse to return to the transmitter to determine its distance from the object. The LRF unit receives its position information from the GPS system and combines the distances found in its laser ranging process with its location to produce a three dimensional map.

Position Tracking

Position tracking is the process of continuously receiving a position, which identifies the location of a device or person. Position tracking services include fleet management, workforce location tracking, automatic vehicle location (AVL), and asset tracking. These may require additional systems to transmit the data to a central location.

Fleet Management

Fleet management is the dispatching, routing and tracking of vehicles to provide shipment or other services that involve the transport of materials and people. For example, rental cars can (and some do) use GPS tracking to determine where their cars have traveled to enforce rental agreements and to determine if the users have been exceeding the speed limit (driving recklessly).

Workforce Location Tracking

Workforce location tracking is the ability of a company or employer to track the location of employees or contractors. Workforce location tracking can be enabled by the GPS receivers that are built into mobile telephones.

Emergency Location Services

Emergency location service is the provision of communication services for a need that is unforeseen by the service provider.

Enhanced 911 is a feature of the landline telephone calling system that provides an emergency dispatcher with the address and number of the telephone used by a user who initiates a call for help. The E911 system has the capability of transferring callers to local police, fire, and ambulance agencies that are within their regional calling area. Emergency calling location information is sent to a public safety answer point (PSAP). PSAPs are facilities that receive and process emergency calls. The PSAP usually receives the calling number identification information. The PSAP operator will then initiate and/or route calls to assist with the emergency situation.

For mobile phones, key issues for location information include where the user is currently located and which PSAP should receive the emergency call. To address these issues, the mobile telephone system obtains position information from the phone. Mobile phone position location can be performed in several ways, including through the use of GPS or through signal triangulation. When the position location of the mobile phone is obtained, it is sent to an automatic location identification (ALI) database. The ALI database function identifies and provides the location of a mobile telephone that has called an emergency number (911) to the PSAP.

Figure 1.23 shows how mobile communication systems can be enhanced through the use of GPS technology to provide for emergency location services. This example shows that a mobile telephone has both mobile communication and GPS reception capability. When the user needs emergency assistance, the GPS information can be sent to the automatic location identification (ALI) database which the public safety access point (PSAP) uses. The mobile system then sends the call with the location information to the PSAP which can display on a map.

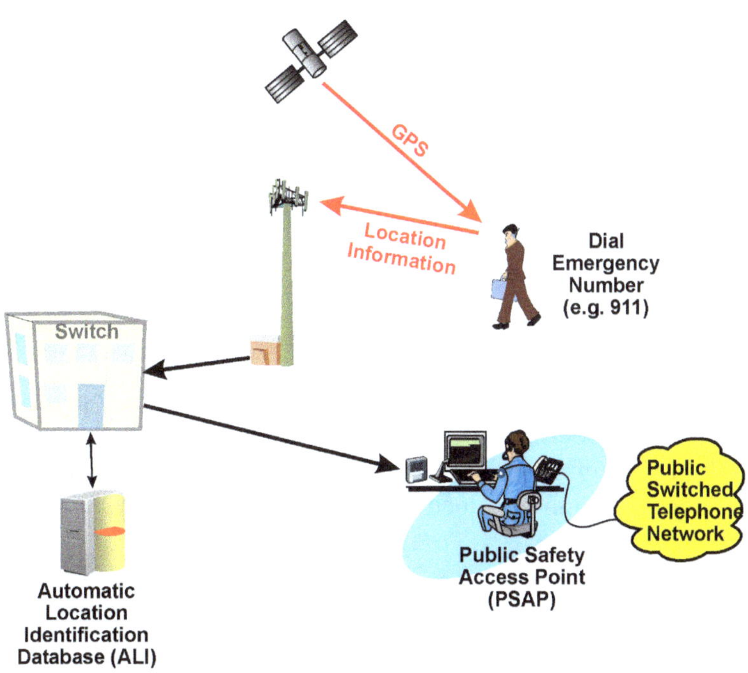

Figure 1.23, Mobile Emergency Location Services

Automated Vehicle Location (AVL)

Automatic vehicle location is a process that can determine the location of a vehicle as it moves within a given geographic area.

Asset Tracking

Asset tracking is the process of determining the location and or status of an item or asset. Asset tracking can be used to monitor the location and condition of shipping containers and valuable equipment or objects.

Agriculture Control

Agriculture control is the monitoring, analysis and assignment of work to manage or improve the cultivation of land or the raising of livestock.

Precision Farming

Precision farming is the use of technology to assist in the optimization of farm production. The technologies used in precision farming range from determining the location of soil samples using GPS signals to the automatic sensing of the conditions and location of farm animals.

Navigation

Navigation is the processes that are used to determine and select routes or paths that can lead to a desired location. GPS navigation services include marine, air, vehicle, personal and automated machine guidance. A key advantage to using the GPS system is that it allows for the continuous updating of location which can be used to track and maintain course headings.

Marine Navigation

Marine navigation is the process of locating, managing and guiding marine vessels through waterways.

Air Navigation

Air navigation is the process of locating, managing and guiding aircraft through airways. Aerial guidance systems are a combination of equipment and software that can sense or determine the location of an aircraft and automatically adjust or define the required adjustments to the motion of the aircraft using the position location information (such as provided from a GPS or INS) and desired destination information. Precise air navigation may be used to assist in aerial refueling, which is the process of connecting a hose between aircraft to transfer fuel between the aircraft.

Vehicle Navigation

Vehicle navigation is the process of locating, managing and guiding vehicles through roadways or terrain. GPS systems provide location information that can be combined with digital maps to provide travel route information.

Personal Navigation

Personal navigation is the use of position information to assist a person in determining traveling directions (travel map) or to find services or other locations of interest. Personal navigation devices can be combined with information systems to provide location-based services (LBS).

Automated Machine Guidance

Automated machine guidance is the process of automatically adjusting the motion of a machine using position location information (such as from a GPS or land based positioning system).

Navigation Warfare

Navigation warfare is the use of navigation signals for military purposes such as missile guidance, munitions control and troop coordination.

Surveying

Surveying is the process of determining the position of points on the earth, measuring distances between them and using this information for a variety of purposes including the defining of boundaries of land ownership. GPS systems can be used for land boundaries, seismic surveying (geology) and volume surveying (mining material). GPS enables surveying to be performed by a single person.

Cadastral Surveying

Cadastral surveying is the process gathering position location information that is used to define the locations of objects or land boundaries in a geographic area for the purposes of showing ownership and/or the value of the land. Precision GPS systems can be used to identify or install survey monuments. A survey monument is a point that has a known or defined location. Survey monuments may be used as a reference for differential (relative) positioning.

Seismic Surveying

Seismic surveying is the process of gathering subsurface geology information that can be used to estimate or predict the potential for earthquakes or other earth changing activity. GPS receivers can be used in combination with geophone acoustic systems to map subsurface geology. The GPS system provides the primary position reference location to the acoustic energy source. The acoustic signals travel through the surface of the earth and are reflected back to acoustic sensors (geophones), which can capture the variations (attenuation) of the acoustic signals due to the sub terrain variations (oil and caves). Geophones are devices that can sense and communicate (or store in memory) reflected acoustic energy that travels through the land.

Volume Surveying

Volume surveying is the process of gathering location and other information that can be used to determine the volume of an object or area. Volume surveying may be used to determine the amount of material that is available in a mound of earth (such as in mining applications to measure the volume of a mound of material).

Structural Deformation Monitoring

Structure deformation monitoring is the process of monitoring the surface of an object or structure (a bridge or a dam) to determine if it has become depressed into the surface on which it is mounted. Deformation monitoring can be used to detect ground subsidence, which is the movement of the surface of the earth towards the center of the earth. Bridge deformation monitoring is the process of monitoring a surface of a bridge to determine if it has changed shape or if it has become depressed into the surface on which it is mounted. GPS systems can be used to detect structural changes in a bridge. Several GPS receivers are located at various points on a bridge that can be used to detect if the bridge structure begins to change.

Vehicle Traffic Management

Vehicle traffic management is the process of monitoring and adjusting traffic systems (traffic light timing) to improve the overall flow and efficiency of traffic. Vehicle traffic management systems can use GPS information from vehicles (or the mobile phones carried by people in the vehicles) to sense the location and speed of traffic on motorways.

Figure 1.24 shows some of the position location applications that are enabled by the GPS system. This table shows that GPS applications can include mapping, location monitoring, agriculture control, navigation, NAVWAR, surveying and deformation monitoring.

Location Function	Types of Services
Mapping	Airborne Mapping, Seafloor Mapping, Utility Maps and GIS
Position Tracking	Fleet Management, Workforce Tracking, Emergency Location Services, Equipment and Goods (e.g. Shipping Containers)
Agriculture Control	Precision Farming
Navigation	Marine, Air, Vehicle, Personal Navigation, Automatic Machine Guidance
Navigation Warfare (NAVWAR)	Missiles, Munitions and Troop Coordination
Surveying	Cadastral, Seismic and Volume
Deformation Monitoring	Bridges, Buildings and Structures

Figure 1.24, GPS Applications

GPS Application Example

GPS devices in rental cars provide a service to people who are traveling in an unfamiliar city. They gain the freedom to tend to their driving rather than their navigating. The GPS enabled device provides the rental car companies with multiple benefits as well. The offering of automated driving directions provides potential revenue to the company. It may also provide an edge over competitors. However, the most valuable use of GPS for the rental company is the ability to recover cars that are stolen or abandoned. If renters are involved in accidents, the GPS device may have logged the driver's speed at the time of the accident, potentially protecting the company from liability. Renters may sign contracts agreeing that they will not take their cars across state or country lines. Renters who may violate their rental agreement by leaving the state or country contrary to their agreement can easily be discovered through the application of GPS technology.

Referemces:

1 . http://www.gps.gov/systems/gps/space/, 22 May, 2015
2 . http://www.esa.int/Our_Activities/Navigation/The_future_-_Galileo/What_is_Galileo
3 . Galileo Satellite Navigation System, Wikipedia, 23 May 2015.
4 . BeiDou Navigation Satellite System, http://en.wikipedia.org/wiki/BeiDou_Navigation_Satellite_System, 23 May 2015.
5 . "Space Segment", http://www.gps.gov/systems/gps/space/, 24 May 2015
6 . "Space Segment", http://www.gps.gov/systems/gps/space/, 24 May 2015

Appendix 1 - Acronyms

3D Mapping-3 Dimensional Mapping
ACS-Attitude Control System
A-GPS-Assisted Global Positioning System
AOA-Angle of Arrival
AS-Antispoofing
ASF-Additional Secondary Phase Factor
Autonav-Autonomous Navigation
AVL-Automatic Vehicle Location
C/A Code-Clear/Acquisition Code
CCR-Corner Cube Reflector
CDP-Cisco Discovery Protocol
CRINEX-Compact Receiver Independent Exchange Format
CS-Commercial Service
DGPS-Differential Global Positioning Service
DGPS-Differential GPS
Differential LORAN-Differential Long Range Navigation
DOP-Dilution of Precision
DR-Dead Reckoning
EGNOS-European Geostationary Navigation Overlay System
eLORAN-Enhanced Long Range Navigation
EMP-Electromagnetic Pulse
EOF-End Of File
ERR-Error Value
FOC-Full Operational Capability
GAGAN-GPS and GEO Augmented Navigation System
GDOP-Geometric Dilution of Precision
GEO-Geosynchronous Earth Orbit
GeoFencing-Geographic Fencing
GFE-Government Furnished Equipment
GIS-Geographic Information System
GIS-Geographical Information System
Glonass-Global Navigation Satellite System
GNSS-Global Navigation Satellite Systems
GPS-Global Positioning System
GRI-Group Repetition Interval
HDOP-Horizontal Dilution of Precision
HOW-Handover Word
IGS-International GNSS Services
IGSO-Inclined Geosynchronous Earth Orbit
IMU-Inertial Measurement Unit
INS-Inertial Navigation System
IOC-Initial Operational Capability
IODC-Issue of Data Clock
IODE-Issue of Data Ephemeris
IONEX-Ionospheric Map Exchange Format
JD-Julian Day
L2 CL-L2 Civil Long
L2 CM-L2 Civil Moderate
LBS-Location Based Services
LEO-Low Earth Orbit
LIDAR-Light Detection and Ranging
LOP-Line of Position
LORAN-Long Range Navigation
LORAN-C-Long Range Navigation C
LPDE-Local Position Determining Entity
LRF-Laser Range Finder
MCS-Master Control Station

MEO-Medium Earth Orbit
MPC-Mobile Position Center
MTSAT-Multifunction Transportation Satellite System
NAVSTAR-Navigation Satellite Timing and Ranging
NAVWAR-Navigation Warfare
NDGPS-Nationwide Differential Global Positioning Service
NDS-National Defense Strategy
NEMA-0183-National Electrical Manufacturer's Association 0183
OS-Open Service
OTF-On the Fly
OTS-Onboard Time Scale
P-Code-Precise Code
PDE-Position Determining Entity
PDOP-Position Dilution of Precision
PDOP-Positional Dilution of Precision
PDT-Position Determination Technology
PF-Primary Phase Factor
PLS-Position Location System
Postprocessing-Post Processing
PPK-Post Processed Kinematic
PPP-Precise Point Positioning
PPS-Precise Positioning Service
PR-Pseudo-Range
PRC-Pseudorange Corrections
PRN-Pseudorandom Noise Number
Pseudolites-Pseudo-Satellite
PVT-Position Velocity Time
Radar-Radio Detection And Ranging
RINEX-Receiver Independent Exchange Format
RRC-Rate of Change of Pseudorange Corrections
RTCA-Radio Technical Commission for Aeronautics
RTCM-Radio Technical Commission for Maritime Service
RTK-Real Time Kinematic
SA-Selective Availability
SAO-Satellite Antenna Offset
SBAS-Satellite Based Augmentation System
SF-Secondary Phase Factor
SINEX-Station Position and Velocity Solutions
SODAR-Sonic Detection and Ranging
SOG-Speed Over Ground
Solar Hour-Sidereal Hour
SONAR-Sound Navigation and Ranging
SP3-Standard Product 3
SPS-Standard Positioning Service
STS-System Time Scale
SV-Satellite Vehicle
SVN-Space Vehicle Number
TAI-International Atomic Time
TDOA-Time Difference of Arrival
TDOP-Time Dilution of Precision
TEC-Total Electron Content
TOE-Time of Emission
TSF-Time Stamped Frame
TTC-Telemetry Tracking & Control
TTFF-Time to First Fix
UERE-User Equivalent Range Error
UT1-Universal Time 1
UTC-Coordinated Universal Time
VDOP-Vertical Dilution of Precision
WAAS-Wide Area Augmentation System
WADGPS-Wide Area Differential GPS
WRS-WAAS Reference Station

Appendix 2 - Positioning Fundamentals

PS navigation calculations are based on true and magnetic north and south standards. Longitude and latitude coordinate system is utilized to determine points on the Earth.Position annotation is expressed in degrees, minutes and seconds ensure accuracy.Position calculation is achieved using basic mathematics and conversion rates.

Standardized North and South

True North and True South- True North and True South are the geographic points that we use on maps to signify the top and bottom of the Earth as we know it. A direction of North on a map intends to point us to the North Pole. In GPS, navigation adjustments are made to account for magnetic variation and assure directions are referencing True North.

Magnetic North and Magnetic South- Magnetic North and Magnetic South are the directions to which a compass will point when placed level on the Earth. As previously discussed, the Magnetic North Pole is approximately 11 degrees west of True North and is located approximately 1,500 miles away in Northwest Canada. Magnetic North and South also change over time. A century from now, the magnetic poles will shift east and back again as the Earth rotates.

Grid North- Grid North is a national designation of North and South in a country. It is used in Great Britain to define the direction of a grid line which is parallel to the central meridian on the National Grid.

Figure A1 describes longitude lines in positions east and west of 0 degrees. This diagram shows that the International Date Line is located exactly opposite of the Prime Meridian or 180 degrees east and west of Greenwich, England. Longitude lines west of Greenwich are known as degrees west, while those east of Greenwich are known as degrees east.

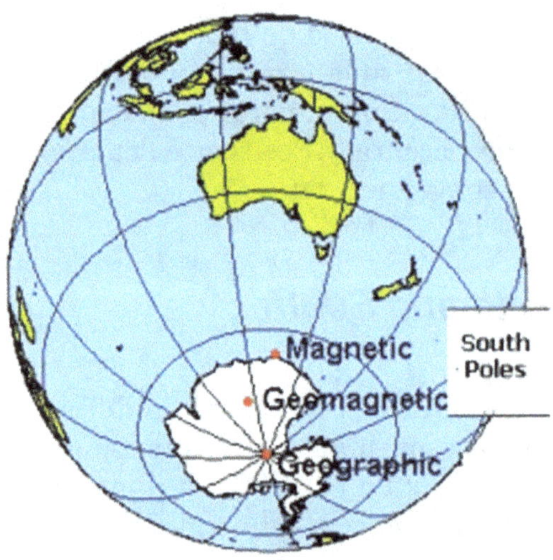

Figure A1, Latitude Longitude

Longitude and Latitude

The standard coordinates systems for identifying points on the Earth are latitude and longitude; a grid like system that identify the intersection of two lines.

Any location on the Earth is described by two numbers: latitude and longitude. The Earth is approximately a sphere (the shape is slightly oval; because of the Earth's rotation, where the equator bulges out a little). For simplicity, imagine a transparent Earth, as a sphere.

The position "P", on Earth can be defined as two angles;

a) The angle between the equator and the position "P". This would define an angle of arc between 0 degrees and 90 degrees. 0 degrees is any position on the equator and 90 degrees defines the North Pole. Angles below the equator can be defined as negative numbers between 0 and 90 degrees. This angle of arc is known as Latitude with -90 degrees being the South Pole.

b) The second angle that can be defined is the point around the equator where the point "P" is found. If the Earth is viewed from above we can view it as a circle that can be divided into 360 degrees. The point P will be found at some point on this circle.

The point where the vertical line crosses "P" and the horizontal lines cross "P" is our unique coordinate. These are standardized as latitude and longitude.

Figure A2 describes a position "P" on the Earth as the point where the vertical and horizontal lines cross (unique coordinate). This diagram shows the coordinates for Position "P" at the surface of the Earth. Point "C" is the center of the Earth.

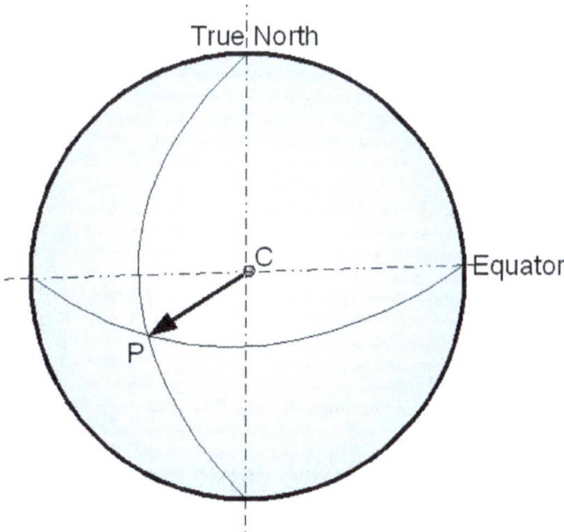

Figure A2, Vector for Position on Earth

Latitude

The globe is marked with parallel lines starting at the equator and ending at the North and South Poles. As shown in the figure below, these horizontal lines are spaced an equal distant from each other. Dividing the distance between the equator and the North Pole by 90 will provide us with one degree of angle per horizontal line. That means each degree of latitude is 111km apart (69 miles). These lines of Latitude (also called "Parallels") are numbered from 0° to 90° north and south. Zero degrees is the equator, (the imaginary line which divides the Earth into the north and south hemispheres. We can repeat the procedure to the south and 90° south marks the South Pole.

Figure A3 shows that the lines of latitude are defines as lines that run parallel to the Equator starting at the North Pole and ending at the South Pole.

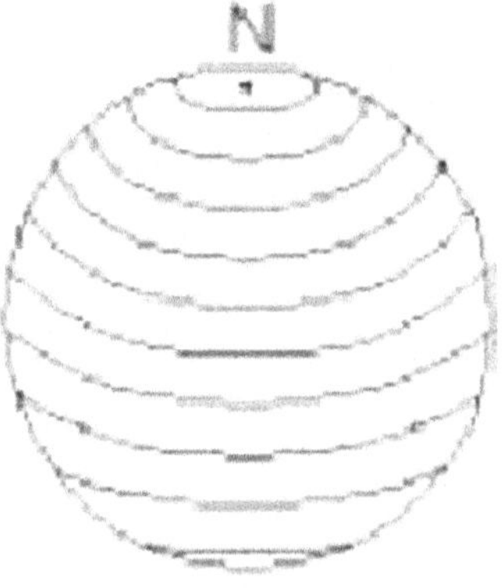

Figure A3, Latitude Lines

Longitude

To define our lines of longitude we can draw lines between the North and South Pole, dividing the Earth into 360 pieces. Each Longitude line or "Meridian" line is defined as a degree of arc (east or west). The issue is only to decide which line is 0 degrees. By historical decision, 0 degrees is the longitude line that passes through the Royal Astronomical Observatory in Greenwich, England. This longitude line is also known as the 0 meridian (or Prime Meridian or the Rose Line) and is our reference point.

Figure A4 shows that the lines of longitude are defined as lines that run from the North Pole to the South Pole.

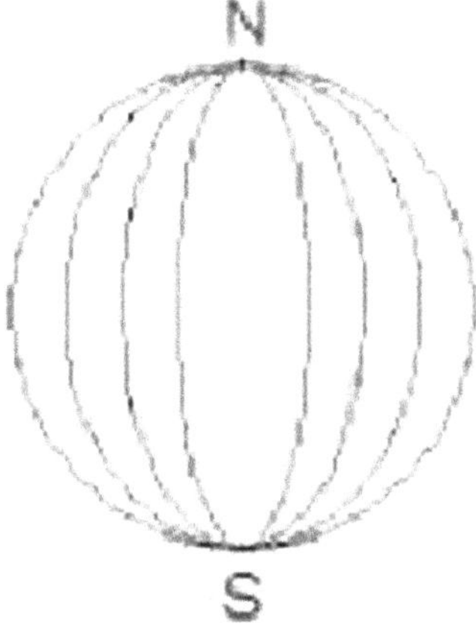

Figure A4, Longitude Lines

Rather than simply number the angles 0°-359°, the degrees that are east of the Zero Meridian are numbered from up to 180° and annotated as: "East". Moving West from Greenwich, England the angles are numbered to 180° "West". The point where they meet in the Pacific Ocean is what is defined as the International Date Line as established in 1884.

The coordinate system

The coordinate system is the process that is used to reference any point "P" on the globe by its unique coordinates (longitude and latitude). This is the exact system used for GPS. Any point on the Earth is defined as two angles; the latitude, the degrees of arc above or below the Equator, and the longitude, the degrees east or west of the Prime Meridian.

Increasing Accuracy

As noted previously, a degree of angle for latitude is 69 miles, which doesn't necessarily lend itself for turn by turn navigation. To make the system more accurate, degrees (shown as "°") can be divided into minutes (60 minutes per degree) and is denoted by a single quote mark ('). Those minutes can be divided to seconds and shown as a double quote. (")
Longitude changes with movement north and south; therefore a definite conversion from degrees to meters cannot be provided.

Figure A5 shows the conversion of angles into miles and meters. This diagram shows that an angle of one degree is equal to 69 miles and 111 km. One minute is equivalent to 1.2 miles and 1.85 km. This figure also shows that one second is equal to 101 ft and 19 m, while one tenth of a second converts to 10 ft or 2 m.

Angle	Miles	Meters
One Degree	69 miles	111 km
One Minute	1.2 miles	1.85 km
One Second	101 feet	19 m
1/10 second	10 ft	2 m

Figure A5, Latitude Facts Table

Figure A6 shows that the symbol for degrees is °, the symbol for minutes is ', and the symbol for seconds is ".

Increasing Accuracy by using decimal notation

For computational purposes and increasing accuracy of coordinates, the traditional angles shown in degrees, minutes and seconds are shown in decimal form.

Symbol for degrees	°
Symbol for minutes	'
Symbol for seconds	"

Figure A6, degrees, minutes, seconds

The computation for this is simple but is often done erroneously because we forget that the coordinates latitude and longitude ("lat/long") are angular numbers and are degrees of arc. For this reason, in order to convert minutes and seconds to a decimal form, we must recall that:

1 degree is 1/360th of a circle
1 minute is 1/60th of a degree (.016667)
1 second is 1/60th of a minute (.000278)

By convention, when using the decimal form of latitude, the number is positive for positions above the equator and negative for positions below the equator. For longitude, positions west of 0 degrees (the Prime Meridian) are shown as negative numbers and positions east of the Prime Meridian at Greenwich, England, are shown as positive numbers.
Let's take an example of converting between the two formats.

Figure A7 shows the latitude and longitude of Howland Island. This diagram shows its latitude is slightly north of the equator. At 48 minutes and 18 seconds above the equator it is just under the 1 degree parallel. This example also shows that the island is west of the Prime meridian by 176 degrees. Since the International Date Line is at 180 degrees, it can be

Place	Latitude	Longitude
Howland Island	*0° 48' 18" N*	*176° 37' 12" W*

Figure A7, Howland Island Coordinates

inferred that the point is in the Pacific Ocean nearly at the International Date Line.

To convert the latitude to a decimal form is a simple matter of multiplication and addition:
0 degrees is left as an integer 0
48 minutes is 48 * 1/60 0.800
18 seconds is 18 * 1/60 * 1/60 0.005
The decimal equivalent is the sum 0.805
This is shown as a positive number

To convert the longitude to decimal form the same method is used:
176 degrees west is left as an integer 176
37 minutes is 37 * 1/60 0.617
12 seconds is 12 * 1/60 * 1/60 0.003
The decimal equivalent is the sum 176.620
This number is negative (west) -176.620

The reverse calculations are simple as well. To convert a decimal representation of latitude to angles of arc:
Latitude 0.085 is taken as an integer 0 degrees
Divide remainder into minutes .085/(1/60) 48.3 mins
Take remainder of whole minutes 0.3
Divide to find seconds 0.3/(1/60) 18 seconds
Since the number is positive, the position is north of the Equator.
Latitude is converted to decimals as 0° 48' 18 "N

The longitude is shown as -176.620.
In a similar fashion:
Longitude -176.620 as an integer -176 degrees
Divide remainder into minutes .620/(1/60) 37.2 mins
Take remainder of whole minutes 0.2
Divide to find seconds 0.2/(1/60) 12 seconds
The longitude is shown as a negative number west (of 0°, the Prime Meridian)
Longitude is converted to decimals as 176° 37' 12"W

Figure A8 shows the longitude and latitude lines that cover the continent of North America, which make up a grid formation, enabling any group of coordinates to be used for location determination purposes.

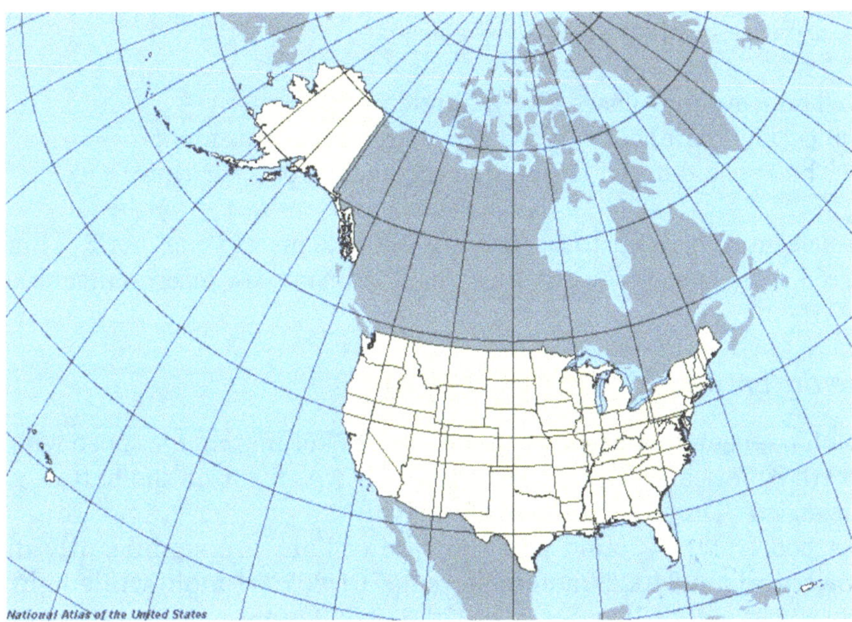

Figure A8, Coordinates

Rate, Time and Distance

For those who are math phobic, this formula is the total extent of the math that is required to understand GPS.

Quite simply, if traveling at a rate of 60 miles per hour for one hour it can be calculated that the time traveled is 60 miles.

In order for GPS to determine location, the same principals are used. The relationship between time, distance and speed (rate) is essential to navigation and GPS. Location technologies have matured, yet the basic math remains the same. Position determination

Rate x Time = Distance

Time:The time that passes for a single measurement
Distance:The distance traveled for a single measurement
Rate:The speed defined as the distance achieved over time

A vesicle may be said to be driving 100 kilometers per hour. This can be referred to as speed, velocity or rate. The terms are interchangeable.

Time differential of Arrival (TDOA)

If you have been to a baseball game, (or cricket match, for those who are not in North America or Japan), and your seat was far from the batter, you have experienced "Time Differential of Arrival".
The speed (rate) of sound and the rate of light are significantly different. Sound travels at 340.29 meters/second (761.207051 mph) while light travels at the speed of 299,792,458 m/s (670,616,629 mph)

When the batter strikes the ball, both the image (light) of the event and the sound of the event start their journey towards you. Since light travels faster, you actually see the bat hit the ball before you hear the sound of the bat hitting the ball. Since you are at a fixed distance from the event, this is expected because time it will take for the image (light) to arrive at your eyes and before the sound arrives at your ears. Knowing the speed of light, the speed of sound and the distance from the batter you can calculate the time it will take each the light and sound to reach you simply by TIME = Distance/Rate. But in our situation, we do not know the distance between our seats and the action. How can we calculate our distance without knowing it? The one piece of data we have to work with is the time between the arrival of the light and the arrival of the sound.

The difference in the time of travel is known as the time differential of arrival (TDOA). You can calculate your distance from the batter by timing the period between the arrival of the light and the arrival of the sound. Since:Rate x Time = Distance and the distance that both sound and light will travel is the same (D, Distance), we can say that Speed of Sound x Time Traveled = Speed of Light x Time Traveled

Let's solve this problem to understand TDOA.Our dilemma is that we don't know how long the light or the sound traveled. We only know the difference. If we heard the crack of the bat two seconds after we saw the bat strike the ball, we know we have a differential of two seconds, thus:
Time of travel of Sound=Time of travel of Light + 2 seconds

At what distance does light and sound have a time differential of 2 seconds? We can do some algebra or we can simply use an easy method and create a table, as would a GPS system. We can create a table that will plug in different values for Distance, until we find a time differential of two seconds (from our example.)

Since Rate x Time = Distance, then Time=Distance/Rate.

Figure A9 shows the calculation of distance from the batter using time differential of arrival. This diagram has converted miles per hour to feet per second. It is unknown how far away from the batter at the baseball game (or cricket match) we are sitting but we do know that the time difference between the time we saw the ball strike the bat and the time our ear heard the impact was two seconds (in this example). This table calculates increasing values of distance until we find a distance that shows a time of arrival of light and sound that differ by two seconds.

Note that the column marked "Differential" is shown with no decimal places. This is accurate because in any mathematical calculation we cannot achieve a result that is more precise than our least precise value. Since our values for distance and the speed of light are integers, our results can not be more accurate than an integer.

Distance Calculation via Time Differential of Arrival

Distance	Light		Sound		Differential
(feet)	Rate (ft/sec)	Time Traveled (secs)	Rate (ft/sec)	Time Traveled (sec)	(seconds)
500	983,571,056	0.0000005084	1116.43701	0.44785	0
600	983,571,056	0.0000006100	1116.43701	0.53742	1
700	983,571,056	0.0000007117	1116.43701	0.62699	1
800	983,571,056	0.0000008134	1116.43701	0.71657	1
900	983,571,056	0.0000009150	1116.43701	0.80614	1
1,000	983,571,056	0.0000010167	1116.43701	0.89571	1
1,100	983,571,056	0.0000011184	1116.43701	0.98528	1
1,200	983,571,056	0.0000012200	1116.43701	1.07485	1
1,300	983,571,056	0.0000013217	1116.43701	1.16442	1
1,400	983,571,056	0.0000014234	1116.43701	1.25399	1
1,500	983,571,056	0.0000015251	1116.43701	1.34356	1
1,600	983,571,056	0.0000016267	1116.43701	1.43313	1
1,700	***983,571,056***	***0.0000017284***	***1116.43701***	***1.52270***	***2***
1,800	983,571,056	0.0000018301	1116.43701	1.61227	2
1,900	983,571,056	0.0000019317	1116.43701	1.70184	2
2,000	983,571,056	0.0000020334	1116.43701	1.79141	2
2,100	983,571,056	0.0000021351	1116.43701	1.88098	2

Figure A9, Distance from the Batter

The results showed that we are sitting 1,700 feet away from the action. This is a remarkable result. Yes, it's remarkable that we can see the game from a 1/3 of a mile away, but more remarkable is that we are able to so easily determine our distance with so little data.

Time differential of arrival is used in GPS to determine your location. Radio waves travel through space at a fixed rate. Using this fact, it is possible to determine your distance from a satellite based on the time it takes for a radio signal to reach you. In GPS we are told where the satellite is located and when it was at that position. We also know the current time. We must determine our distance from the satellite based on the time difference between transmission of the signal and reception of the signal.

Given that the satellite is at a know altitude in space (25,000 miles) and the speed of radio waves is known the same techniques can be applied to determine your position. This is the magic of GPS.

Radio waves travel at a speed of 186,000 miles per second or 300,000,000 meters per second in space. This is the figure we can use in GPS. Many conditions will slow the waves as they enter the Earth's atmosphere (barometric pressure, weather) but these are not significant enough to concern the science of GPS. Since we are concerned with "differential" reception of satellite signal to a receiver, all signals will be slowed at the same rate and cancel any minor anomalies.

Relative Positions and Speeds

Your position is relative to a fix that you determine. Columbus sailed out of Saltes near Palos, Spain. This was his known position and he had no other points of reference to determine his location as he sailed west across the unexplored Atlantic. Columbus could only know his position relative to his starting point. Today, maps are highly accurate and few points on Earth are unknown. We generally wish to determine our position on a map as our "fix" and then determine directions to a destination.

Rate, as well is relative. The Earth spins at approximately 1,000 miles per hour (at the equator) and travels around the sun at about 67,000 miles per hour. A teenager lying on the coach is viewed by his parents as being stationary, but relative to the sun, he's moving pretty fast. For most of our applications we are concerned with our speed relative to the surface of the Earth. As you wait for a traffic light to change to green, the Earth below you and the car you sit in are moving. In relationship to the Sun and stars, however for the purposes of our discussions we take our speed (rate) to be zero when we are stationary on Earth.

Driving at 70 miles per hour across the United States, we are referencing to our speed relative to the ground beneath us. The concept of relative speed and relative position is very important in the design of the GPS system because we are using a system of satellites that are in orbit around the

Earth and furthermore are traveling in multiple directions around the Earth, which itself is spinning at 1,000 MPH and is in a 365 day orbit around the Sun.

Consider when you travel in an airplane. The airplane is traveling over the spinning Earth but is traveling at 700 MPH in reference to the ground, while you walk around the airplane at 1 or 2 miles per hour relative to the floor of the airplane. What is GPS to do?

For the purposes of GPS, any stationary point on Earth is considered to be a fix that is traveling at 0 MPH.

The concepts of relative position and relative rate of speed become very important in GPS because, as you will read, the system depends on satellites in motion and in orbit over the Earth.

Triangulation

Triangulation is a well know method of determining ones location if you can determine your distance from known locations. Lighthouses, Airport beacons and Cellular towers are all used for assisting navigators find their way. An example is the easiest way to explain triangulation. Imagine that you are lost on a large golf course. You have a map of the course and a small telescope that some golfers use to determine their distance to the hole. (It measures the relative height of the flag on the Green and helps some golfers plan their approach.). How can you find out, where on the walking path you are?Triangulation allows you to do this quickly.

Figure A10 is an example of how triangulation enables location determination. Using a telescope the flag for Hole 8 is spotted, and determined to be 300 yards away. Circle (A) is drawn around Hole 8 with a radius of 300 yards. Flag 7 is measured at 100 yards from position. Circle (B) is drawn with a radius of 100 yards. This circle intersects circle A at two points. The position must be one of two points (A, B)on the golf course. To complete the triangulation, one more point of reference is needed. A final flag is selected measuring 75 yards away. Drawing a circle (C) around the flag at hole 15

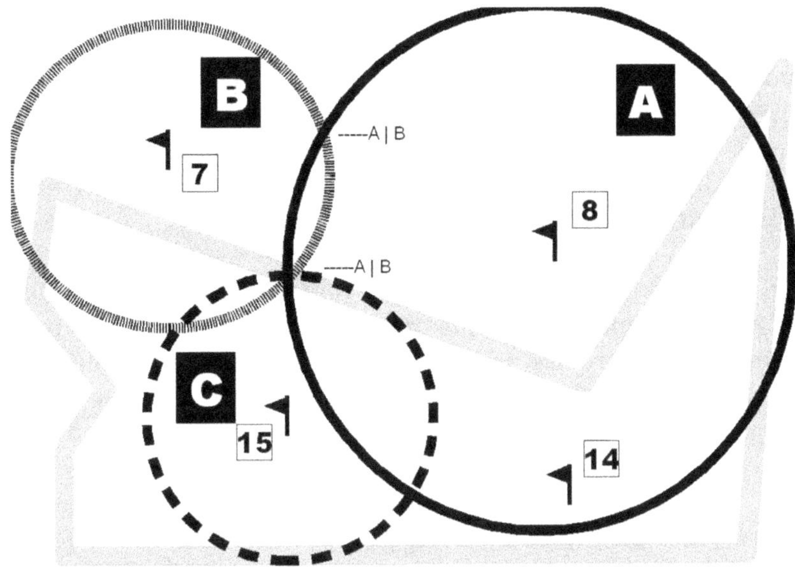

Figure A10, Triangulation Example

with a radius of 75 yards determines that it intersects the (A) and (B) circles at the lower A|B point. This diagram shows that one can successfully determine position based on triangulation and process of elimination.

Note that it didn't matter which three flags you selected, the triangulation would have resulted in the same answer. It is also important to note that the small telescope we are using may not be perfectly accurate therefore our three circles may not intersect perfectly. In these cases, we can improve our accuracy by taking more measurements and using the average location of the intersection of four or five measurements. GPS uses triangulation to determine the location of a users device by measuring it's distance to satellite's that have a known location.

GPS uses techniques and methods similar to those used in the time of Columbus. Known time standards are used. Rather than measure the time it takes a log to move a known distance, GPS uses the time radio waves travel from satellites in space that have a known distance from Earth. By determining the time it takes radio signals to travel from artificial stars, (known as man made satellites) and reach the receivers, the receivers' location can be known. Multiple satellites with known positions enable extremely accurate position determinations.

Since GPS can make measurements in a matter of milliseconds when fully warmed up, it can make multiple measurements at regular intervals in order to provide very precise navigation and also determine the velocity and acceleration of a GPS unit. If you know your position at regular intervals over a short period of time you can determine your velocity at any given time as well as your acceleration (your change in speed).

Given any two factors, you can determine the third and thus determine your position if you have a fourth element; a known position. Remember, above all, positions and rates are relative.

Index

www.ingramcontent.com/pod-product-compliance
Lightning Source LLC
LaVergne TN
LVHW080311110826
845155LV00023B/117
* 9 7 8 1 9 3 2 8 1 3 1 9 7 *